Renewing Professional Librarianship

Renewing Professional Librarianship

A Fundamental Rethinking

BILL CROWLEY

Beta Phi Mu Monograph Series
Art Young, Series Editor

LIBRARIES
UNLIMITED
A Member of the Greenwood Publishing Group

Westport, Connecticut • London

Library of Congress Cataloging-in-Publication Data

Crowley, William A., 1949–
  Renewing professional librarianship : a fundamental rethinking / Bill Crowley.
    p. cm.—(Beta Phi Mu monograph series)
  Includes bibliographical references and index.
  ISBN 978-1-59158-554-1 (alk. paper)
 1. Library science—United States. 2. Library science—Canada. 3. Library educa-
tion. 4. Library schools—Accreditation. 5. Librarians—Certification. 6. Libraries—
Aims and objectives. I. Title.
  Z665.2.U6C76   2008
  020.973—dc22   2007042429

British Library Cataloguing in Publication Data is available.

Library of Congress Catalog Card Number: 2007042429
ISBN: 978-1-59158-554-1
ISSN: 1041-2751

First published in 2008

Libraries Unlimited, 88 Post Road West, Westport, CT 06881
A Member of the Greenwood Publishing Group, Inc.
www.lu.com

Printed in the United States of America

The paper used in this book complies with the
Permanent Paper Standard issued by the National
Information Standards Organization (Z39.48–1984).

10 9 8 7 6 5 4 3 2 1

This work is dedicated, with gratitude, to my spouse Theresa Van Gundy Crowley, a most admirable human being whose first-rate mind and willingness to share her acute understandings of human nature, when heeded, have so often worked to my advantage. I am ever so deeply in her debt.

Contents

Acknowledgments

THIS BOOK WOULD NOT HAVE been written without the valuable assistance of two strong sources of support. The first was the encouragement provided by the many American and Canadian librarians, particularly my friends in British Columbia, who on a daily basis demonstrate the value of professional librarianship. To a great degree, this work is their story. The second source of encouragement and assistance was the Beta Phi Mu Monograph Editorial Board. Under the leadership of Art Young, the board members repeatedly contributed sage advice and remarkable professional understandings that simply made for a better book. Naturally, any remaining problems or issues are the responsibility of the author.

CHAPTER 1

Introduction

SCENARIO: A "LIBRARY" EDUCATION STORY

Several years ago Deborah Ginsberg and the author were delivering a presentation on the future of librarianship before a late-afternoon audience at the small but significant Ethics of Electronic Information in the 21st Century symposium, held for years in Memphis, Tennessee. As the last presenters of the day we were allowed a little extra time to describe how the emphasis on seeing librarians as merely information intermediaries, a problematic classification that is increasingly characteristic of American Library Association (ALA)–accredited programs, was having discernibly negative impacts on the career prospects of library practitioners. One of the themes was that the slighting of the librarian's roles in the broad areas of culture, specifically the important areas of education, and entertainment has helped to generate a climate where employers are comfortable replacing librarians, now defined as but one part of the information infrastructure (Rubin 2004) with less educated and, consequently, less expensive staff (Crowley and Ginsberg 2002).

At this assertion a British academic, another symposium presenter who was sitting in the audience, rose to point out what he saw as an obvious benefit for embracing the primacy of information—program survival in the academic world. Just a few years before his own library program had been losing so many students that its parent institution was considering closing it down, with a consequent loss of faculty jobs. Through a deliberate decision to switch the program's emphasis from the preparation of "librarians" to the education of "information specialists," the faculty and administration had tapped into the corporate market, changed the program's image, and turned things around. The program's student enrollment drastically increased, significant research funding began to appear, and faculty positions were preserved. This story led to additional comments from other faculty members sitting in the audience, some from other countries but many employed by ALA-accredited programs. For the most part their remarks extolled the many benefits, some rising to the level of virtues, of a library program "going informational."

A position contrary to this information celebration was expressed in private by a senior academic librarian who cornered the author after the session. Frowning at the news she had to convey, this individual confessed that the profession's very public equation of librarian with information, coupled with the availability of associate degree and bachelor's degree holders who had been taught to view themselves as information providers, had allowed her institution's administrators to downsize the professional librarian component of the library workforce.

"Obviously, redefining professional positions downward doesn't do too much for professionalism. But it is a way we can show how we are doing more with less," she pointed out, echoing one of the business model catchphrases popular at the turn of the twentieth century.

The reality that making the "information turn" has allowed ALA-accredited programs to grab a greater share of the corporate and research market for information specialists, knowledge managers, and competitive data analysts is undeniable. More controversial is that embracing information as an unalloyed good obscures the downside of an information education for the very same academic, public, and school library communities which, generations ago, took the lead with legislators and university administrators to bring the educators' very own ALA-accredited programs into existence. There is a long-standing maxim of American pragmatism that the solution to a current problem is often the next problem to be solved. To build on some of the information ethics concepts that the Memphis symposium has long sought to promote, the negative consequences flowing from equating "librarian" with "information provider" have become the new problem in the library field. It is appropriate to accept the good intentions of those involved in this transformation. Consequently, their failure to examine the negative consequences—such as the encouragement of librarian deprofessionalization—resulting from the conversion of library schools into information programs is likely to have another explanation than a systematic bias against all things "library." The reality may be that the mental models given to information educators through their own graduate education are inadequate for addressing library realities. The profoundly destructive implications of this disconnection, something to be expected when one academic area (information) applies its models to educating practitioners for a separate field of study (librarianship), will be further addressed in the various chapters of this work.

THE PURPOSE OF THIS BOOK

The purpose of *Renewing Professional Librarianship: A Fundamental Rethinking* is simply stated. This book is written as an exploration of how professional librarianship can be safeguarded and enhanced in the new millennium. Briefly summarized, it offers a vision of librarian professionalism grounded in human learning, something that the author chooses to term *lifecycle librarianship* and, half in jest, has defined as providing library services from "the lapsit to the nursing home." The concept of lifecycle librarianship is rooted in librarianship's fundamental commitment to promoting lifelong learning. It is, in short, educational. As such it offers an option for envisioning library education, services, and programs that contrasts with the business model and the concentration on the information life cycle that are fundamental components within the field of information science. The information science paradigm or meta-model of the world redefines professional librarianship, indeed "defines it down" as a minor player in the information universe. In consequence, since information science does not privilege the values and multiple responsibilities of librarianship, it sees the field as populated by individuals who are simply minor parts of a globalized information reality. It offers no intellectual support for defending the careers of professional librarians and may indeed encourage their replacement by the less expensive human options whose information educations were provided in associate degree information technology or undergraduate information programs.

This Beta Phi Mu monograph was written to remind professionals and educators that there is an alternative view of librarianship, library science, or library studies—the terms will be used interchangeably—for academic, public, and school librarians that both illuminates current experience and is grounded in library history. It is a commonsense response to the reality that when much of the world seems to be adopting a self-service approach to acquiring information online, the "library equals information" model does not seem to promise much of a future for professional librarianship. As already noted the author has tentatively termed this alternative vision of professionalism life-cycle librarianship and sees it as providing a more stable and more re-alistic intellectual foundation for understanding what professional academic, public, and school librarians actually do, and why they are or can be valued by their service communities.

One underlying premise of this work is that the life span of the transitional area of study that some term "library and information sci-ence," what ALA defines as "library and information studies" (ALA 1992), has been declared "over" by information theorists who simply ignore "library" and discuss "information." In its twenty-five- to thirty-year history, the now disintegrating field educated quite a number of practitioners and did yeoman work in helping make "information" a sometimes respectable area of study in academic environments. However, since "library" has all but been eliminated from explana-tions of the term (ALA 1992), it now confuses rather than clarifies. Accumulating realities of both off-campus and academic practice demonstrate that we now have two fields. The newer field, what some would see as librarianship's daughter area of study, is information sci-ence. Unfortunately, information science, for reasons often involving income and prestige as well as more intellectual sources of opposition, refuses to admit the continued viability of the library, parent disci-pline. At best, the library world is assigned a minor supporting role in the information universe.

As will be seen, the ability of information science to claim that library science is but a part of its field flows from the reality that there are obvious areas of overlap (Saracevic 1999). For example, academic, public, and school libraries provide information while even corporate information centers occasionally support some type of instruction. While all analogies have their weaknesses, the distinction between library science and information science parallels the generally ac-knowledged differences separating *public administration,* with its con-centration on government and not-for-profit organizations, and *busi-ness administration,* with its commitment to profit-oriented concerns. The fields of library science and information science differ so much at their cores, with librarianship concentrating on learning and informa-tion science concerned with information, that they should rightly be considered to have an equally separate status.

Within the domains studied by public administration and business administration there is also a certain amount of shared intellectual space and it is possible for the holder of a master of public administration or master of business administration degree to be educated in one area and successfully employed in the other. However, the bulk of what practitioners do in each field is sufficiently different to require separate educations and distinct majors or degrees, whether the programs are offered together in a college of management or are located in separate academic units. Degrees in public administration, for example, are often offered as part of a political science program. In this context, it must be stressed that the *Chronicle of Higher Education*—the "house organ" of the university world—lists the number of degrees annually awarded in business administration and public administration as part of the separate compilations titled "business, management, and marketing" and "public administration and social-service professions" ("Earned Degrees Conferred 2003–4" 2006). Keeping the business administration–public administration distinction in mind provides a useful yardstick (meterstick) for considering the differences between the fields alternately termed "library science" or "librarianship" and the field labeled "information science" or "information."

Librarians, particularly academic, public, and school librarians, are now facing the very real prospect of having their profession redefined out of existence, in part because of an inappropriate subordination under the information model (Apostle and Raymond 1997). This situation is not the result of what some see as a malevolent conspiracy, a cabal of information faculty forming the proverbial fifth column to subvert programs of professional library education by undermining the very concept of librarianship from within (Gorman 2000). Rather, within the United States, it represents the cumulative byproduct of decisions made, often with the best of intentions, by

- educators concerned about the survival of their ALA-accredited programs, intrigued by information issues, mesmerized by the lure of the growing information economy, or seemingly fed up with discussing the concerns of libraries (Cronin 1995);
- university and school administrators driven by demands for cost containment and the potential for enhanced prestige and revenue;
- public library managers implementing the information-oriented "business model," in part to achieve national rankings; and
- practitioners who have been taught no alternative to the increasingly less viable definition of librarian as information provider.

Although disputed (Cronin 2000; Saracevic 1994), the task of insuring that professional librarians receive an appropriate education has long been deemed to be the province of ALA. For reasons to be discussed, it has become clear that the association has failed in its task and that the process of ALA accreditation itself will need to be reformed. This effort will require leadership by academic, public, and school library associations on state and national levels to bring community and/or institutional stakeholders together to identify the knowledge, understanding, and skill needed by professional librarians in various contexts. In the process, the effort will also provide ALA with the blueprint to insure that present or alternative accredited programs offer courses and degrees that embody and convey such requirements.

It is time to tone down the combative rhetoric (Cronin 1995; Dillon and Norris 2005; Gorman 2000) and seek solutions that, ideally, safeguard both practitioner and faculty interests. In all fairness, before the various elements of the library community justly demand appropriate education from the preferred vendors of master's degrees accredited by ALA, it is necessary to identify what academic, public, and school libraries—the historic heart of librarianship—actually do. Similarly, it may be appropriate for the former areas of librarianship that have been absorbed by information science—such as corporate knowledge management and competitive data analysis—to undertake a similar approach to providing relevant education for that newer field. In this context, the conditions under which ALA is accrediting appropriate library education even in information programs will need to be specified.

The highly diverse programs of information education are unlikely to ever agree to create a "stand-alone" process of program accreditation. For years, a number of fields and disciplines have accredited some form of information education (Galvin 1992) and the imperatives of finance and disciplinary jealousy, as well as university resentment against the demands of accrediting bodies, are likely to work against creating a new system. However, as the fields of library science and information science solidify, again with occasional overlap, information science advocates will need to take a leadership role in assuring that a library association—ALA—sets appropriate criteria for providing its stamp of approval for the separate information science field. This approach will bring with it the possibility, even the necessity, of all ALA-accredited programs offering degrees containing two majors, providing separate degrees (as is now occasionally done), or devising otherwise acceptable methods of providing the educations appropriate to the distinct library and information domains.

THE AUTHOR'S RESEARCH PHILOSOPHY

The intellectual approach taken to exploring the misapplication of information models to the predominately learning-centered realities of professional academic, public, and school librarianship reflects the author's adherence to cultural pragmatism, described in some depth in the recent *Spanning the Theory-Practice Divide in Library and Information Science* (Crowley 2005). Fundamental to classical pragmatism and the more contemporary variant of cultural pragmatism is the assertion that the true test of any theory lies in the ongoing analysis of experience. However, the way practitioners, including the faculty who "practice" in universities and colleges, actually go about analyzing such experience represents a mixture of objectivity and subjectivity. Claims by one side to a dispute that it is operating objectively while the other side is arguing subjective values (Cronin 1995) are, at best, disingenuous. It is now a mainstream concept to view all individuals as prone to label their values as truth (Neustadt and May 1986). In consequence "truth seeking" can often become an effort to determine and examine which values are in play. Consider, for example, the consequences of the following theory, fundamental to the education offered aspiring professional librarians in master's degree programs accredited by ALA, that everything a library does is part of the information model. If students believe this, they will view their future employment through the information lens. This model functions quite well in corporate and research information and knowledge management centers. However, the claims of information professors that everything is explained by information theory are consistently undermined by the learning realities of academic, public, and school libraries. Increasingly this is being played out as a form of professional cognitive dissonance, defined here as a condition where the theories taught by information educators actually conflict with academic, public, and school library professional realities. To paraphrase a very old joke, it does seem to be the case that information educators are frequently asking professional librarians to believe them and their information models instead of the day-to-day library actualities discerned through their "lying eyes."

Cultural pragmatism can be viewed as a contemporary descendent of the larger philosophy of pragmatism, particularly as pragmatism was advanced in the early twentieth century by the American intellectual giants William James and John Dewey (Crowley 2001, 2005). Cultural pragmatism benefits from the fact it arrived on the scene a century after its "parent" when it could take advantage of newer understandings proposed by theorists, including library and information theorists, who operate from feminist, critical theory, and other philosophical schools and traditions. In researching the foundations of cultural pragmatism, the author found certain ideas from the "classical" pragmatic era (early to mid-twentieth century) were particularly relevant to theorizing on a variety of issues. Here it will be noted that not all classical or contemporary pragmatists might agree with this listing but these understandings still work for author and, pragmatically "speaking," that represents about the best reason to keep using them.

These classical pragmatic understandings, modernized to address the contemporary problems addressed by cultural pragmatism, in this case the relevance of information theory to library practice, include

1. knowledge and meaning are determined by experience
2. research is instigated by a problem
3. ideas are instruments for defining and solving problems
4. philosophy and theory development are human endeavors, subject to human limitations
5. propositions are meaningless unless their being either true or false will make a difference in our lives
6. meanings always require human context; there are no eternal essences or ideal objects
7. theories are, at best, provisionally true and are always subject to further testing in a variety of contexts
8. what counts is not where ideas come from but what we can do with them
9. facts always involve an element of value, and values cannot be conceived in isolation from the world of concrete events
10. any attempt to improve the world must begin by finding out how the world actually works
11. humans have the most opportunity to develop their capabilities in a democracy

12. scientific and other knowledge progresses best in a democratic context that encourages freedom of inquiry (Crowley 2001, 2005).

As the author has noted in previous essays specifically addressing issues affecting the survival of academic librarians (Crowley 1997, 2001), the arguments advanced in *Renewing Professional Librarianship: A Fundamental Rethinking* will need to be tested by the reader to determine if they explain her or his experience. The necessary effort to reform library education will require a sustained effort, the sort of commitment that comes only when people make such a reformation a part of their professional lives at the gut level. With luck it can be achieved, not this year or the next, but most certainly within the next decade. However, it may well ultimately be the case, to adapt a phrase long applied to Chicago politics, that "ALA is not ready for reform."

If restructuring the ALA system of accreditation is not possible, the American library community will probably need to prepare itself for the slow extinction of the concept of professional librarianship defined in part through earning a specific degree. This demise will not be a dramatic event but will extend over a period of years. It will be the predictable result of ALA's bureaucratic and regulatory inertia, program resistance, and the inability of the core library professions to undertake the extended organizational and political battles necessary to insure their professional survival. As information education continues to diverge from library practice pragmatically inclined planners at the state level, within both government and library association circles, will respond to the assertions of practitioners that master's degrees from a program accredited by ALA have become increasingly irrelevant in academic and public library environments (Mulvaney and O'Connor 2006).

State governments do not award degrees, but they do have the power of certification. They will increasingly substitute such certification, even if voluntary, for an accredited library education deemed to be increasingly irrelevant. As a former state division head, the author has experienced how the process works. In response to demands by the library communities of the various states laws will be passed by legislatures to create new certification approaches or to amend systems already in place. Afterward, new or revised regulations will be issued, with a period of time for public comment, by state library agencies to implement the new or revised certification requirements for professional librarians. Academic and public librarians' certification is likely to be voluntary, although it may be required at the level of the individual university or library. In limited circumstances it may be possible to mandate public and perhaps academic librarian certification to parallel the current process for certifying school librarians. Libraries and librarianship will remain but the MLS, MLIS, or IS master's degrees from ALA-accredited programs will lose their already limited attraction as lower educational standards, designed to maximize the number of candidates and reduce personnel costs according to best practice business models, will probably result in lower salaries and a further diminution of librarian prestige.

Even in the electronic information age, Americans still love their libraries, particularly their public libraries. These institutions will survive. However, it is likely that the level of librarian professionalism, as measured by master's degrees from ALA-accredited programs, will decline for academic and public libraries when practitioners revolt against an irrelevant education and the library equivalent of Gresham's Law inevitably becomes operative. As will be recalled from basic economics courses, Gresham's Law describes how "good" money with a greater intrinsic value (intact gold or silver coins) is driven out of circulation by "bad" money (clipped coins or paper bills) whose value as money is intrinsically less (debased coinage) or nonexistent (paper bills) and supported solely or in part by government fiat. Restated in "library" terms, a "bad" professional preparation (easier to obtain, not involving a graduate degree approved by ALA, probably at lower cost, and presumably less intrinsically valuable) drives out "good" professional preparation (harder to obtain ALA-accredited degree, possibly more expensive, and presumably more intrinsically valuable). This is a condition that is likely to come about when both a master's degree from an ALA-accredited program and an alternative state certification are deemed equally acceptable to a state for the educational preparation of professional librarians.

In an environment of limited resources, when state regulations or university policies allow, institutions will be greatly tempted to hire minimally educated librarians who meet state standards and possess desired library skills for less than it would cost to employ candidates whose greater academic preparation increases their cost and limits their availability. Master's degrees from ALA-accredited programs, once potentially seen as equivalent to the MBA and the MSW and accepted as the terminal degree for academic librarians, will be sacrificed as being based on inappropriate information science courses.

ASSUMPTIONS AND ASSOCIATIONS

There are a number of assumptions which lay at the heart of this work.

First, information science is a field of study that is related to but separate from librarianship or library science. It is possible, indeed necessary, to distinguish between these fields in order to assure appropriate professional education for librarianship.

Second, despite the demonstrable differences between library science and information science, the powerful operation of "regulatory capture" (Ehrenhalt 2004)—here defined as control of the ALA accreditation system by the very educational programs it is supposed to regulate—is in the process of allowing information advocates to successfully redefine library education as information education. Although information proponents argue that such a redefinition follows the evidence, less praiseworthy motives cannot be ruled out in all circumstances. It should not be forgotten that restructuring library education as information education provides information schools with a dependable revenue stream based on their accreditation by ALA.

Third, the old definition that library science or librarianship represents a unique field because it has an intellectual domain composed of certain educational, informational, and recreational components is not supported by opinion leaders within the twenty-first century university, even though this definition describes realities encountered by many library practitioners on a daily basis. The situation is obviously unfair, but practitioners need to know that "facts on the ground" are frequently not the most important things in higher education. What is often more significant to professors in ALA-accredited programs are paradigms or meta-models of the world that allow faculty to advance their careers by engaging in the development of theory, securing grants, collaborating across fields and disciplines, and catching the eyes of senior university administrators (Crowley 2005). *Information* is viewed as exactly such a meta-model. *Librarianship*, regardless of the "objective" validity of its claims, is not seen as such by information proponents.

Fourth, although the traditional library intellectual triad of education, information, and recreation is out of favor even within ALA-accredited programs, the paradigm of *education*, redefined by twenty-first-century culture as *learning*, represents a meta-model that is much more descriptive of the work of academic, public, and school librarians than information. As will be seen, the history of librarianship shows that the problems that such professional librarians have been trying to resolve, outside of the obviously information science–oriented concerns of corporate knowledge management and research information centers, are more involved with human learning than with the information life cycle.

Fifth, an emphasis on the learning foundation of library science does not mean that professional librarians do not provide information or assist with what some might see as recreational endeavors. It simply means that these activities are less important to librarianship's understanding of itself than the advancement of human learning.

Sixth, it is highly likely that certain information theorists will try to subsume every learning argument advanced for defining library science as a separate field from information science as evidence that library science is really part of their information model. The author would be disappointed if they did not try to do so. Should they attempt such a redefinition, as they have already successfully done with the old education-information-recreation triad, it will be up to professional librarians to determine whether looking at the world through a learning lens or an information lens best illuminates what they do.

Seventh, the opportunity to reform ALA-accredited professional education has a limited life span. Information education patterns that are detrimental to professional library education are being cemented in place, following patterns found in other "captured" forms of regulation (Faure-Grimaud and Martimort 2003). The prospects for appropriate library education are fast evaporating as a critical mass of information theorists without a library commitment now controls the doctoral programs that ALA is allowing to produce the next generation of information, not library, educators. Given the fact that so many ALA-accredited programs already employ professors who lack a library background and whose doctorates are from other fields, the disappearance of experienced albeit aging "library education" professors will soon set in place an irresistible bias in ALA-accredited programs toward educating librarians as information providers and not librarians.

Here, it is worth reminding readers that the triumph of "information" over "library" may not reflect the achievement of that often elusive value we term "truth" (Neustadt and May 1986). The university world is plagued with trends, and there is some influential theory supporting the view that changes in paradigms or mental models of the world, such as the privileging of information over library may not bring us closer to the "truth" (Kuhn 1970, 170). Professional librarianship based on the model of an ALA-accredited degree may die out, not because such a level of education is unneeded or unwarranted but because changes in the higher education rewards system and, more problematically, boredom with library questions and issues have infected a critical number of information science faculty, making their instruction and research extraneous to practitioner realities.

References

American Library Association. 1992. *Standards for Accreditation of Master's Programs in Library & Information Studies.* Chicago, IL: Office for Accreditation, American Library Association.

Apostle, Richard, and Boris Raymond. 1997. *Librarianship and the Information Paradigm.* Lanham, MD: Scarecrow Press.

Cronin, Blaise. 1995. Shibboleth and substance in North American library and information science education. *Libri,* 45, no. 1 (March): 45–63.

———. 2000. Accreditation: Retool it or kill it. *Library Journal* (15 June): 54.

Crowley, Bill. 1997. The dilemma of the librarian in Canadian higher education. *Canadian Journal of Information and Library Science,* 22, no. 1 (April): 1–18.

———. 2001. Tacit knowledge, tacit ignorance, and the future of academic librarianship. *College & Research Libraries,* 62, no. 6 (November): 565–584.

———. 2005. *Spanning the Theory-Practice Divide in Library and Information Science.* Lanham, MD: Scarecrow Press.

Crowley, Bill, and Deborah Ginsberg. 2002. Intracultural reciprocity, information ethics, and the survival of librarianship in the 21st century. In *Ethics and Electronic Information: A Festschrift for Stephen Almagno.* Jefferson, NC: McFarland & Company.

Dillon, Andrew, and April Norris. 2005. Crying wolf: An examination and reconsideration of the perception of crisis in LIS education. *Journal of Education for Library and Information Science* 46, no. 4 (fall): 280–298.

Earned Degrees Conferred, 2003–4. 2006. *Chronicle of Higher Education* 53, no. 1 (25 August): 22.

Ehrenhalt, Alan. 2004. Assessments: Spreading out the clout. *Governing* (April): 6, 8.

Faure-Grimaud, Antoine, and David Martimort. 2003. Regulatory inertia. *RAND Journal of Economics* 34, no. 3 (autumn): 413–437.

Galvin, Thomas J. 1992. The new ALA standards for accreditation: A personal perspective. *Bulletin of the American Society for Information Science* 18, no. 4 (April/May): 19–20.

Gorman, Michael. 2000. *Our Enduring Values: Librarianship in the 21st Century.* Chicago: American Library Association.

Kuhn, Thomas S. 1970. *The Structure of Scientific Revolutions,* 2nd ed. Chicago: University of Chicago Press.

Mulvaney, John Philip, and Dan O'Connor. 2006. The crux of our crisis. *American Libraries* (June/July), 38–40.

Neustadt, Richard E., and Ernest R. May. 1986. *Thinking in Time: The Uses of History for Decision Makers.* New York: Free Press.

Rubin, Richard E. 2004. *Foundations of Library and Information Science,* 2nd ed. New York: Neal-Schuman.

Saracevic, Tefko. 1994. Closing of library schools in North America: What role accreditation? *Libri* 44, no. 3 (September): 190–200.

——. 1999. Information science. *Journal of the American Society for Information Science* 50, no. 12 (October): 1051–1063.

CHAPTER 2

Librarian Professionalism and Professional Library Education

SCENARIO: TESTIMONY OF A CORPORATE IT REFUGEE

As might be expected, the well-established reputation of Dominican University's Graduate School of Library and Information Science (GSLIS) and its convenient location ten miles from downtown Chicago frequently bring to campus many who are not currently enrolled students. Local librarians, Illinois residents studying in the distance education offerings of other American Library Association–accredited programs, and visiting out-of-town professionals can be found at Dominican with some regularity. Their numbers and activities vary with the rhythms of the academic year, but GSLIS faculty members working in their office with the door open are inevitably deemed to be available for a drop-in visit by students, alums, and even total strangers. About a year ago, between the fall and spring semesters, the author had the unexpected company of a newly minted librarian, a midlife career changer, who was staying with a local friend and had a remarkable story to tell. A self-described "IT corporate refugee," she possessed a long work history in information technology and a degree in computer science. A few years back she had applied to her local ALA-accredited program after being compelled to train her successor—under pain of immediate termination and a poor reference—when her corporate management decided to "offshore" her job to Bangalore, India.

Disabused of the claims for a future without limits in corporate information technology (IT) and interested in an academic or public library position that was not likely to be shipped overseas, this unexpected winter visitor told a tale of enrolling in a program offering an ALA-accredited master's degree and almost changing her mind the day of its orientation for new students. As she reported, during the introductory session the younger faculty in the room spoke with passion of the world of "information science" and "informatics" and referred to those in attendance not as potential librarians but as aspiring "information practitioners." These same faculty members, she recalled, spoke about "librarianship" and "librarians" only in historical terms.

Irritated by this proselytizing for information science, a field she disdained as "computer science light" and that was also subject to being offshored to any nation with a sufficient supply of English speakers and online access to databases, this visitor recalled how she had started eying the exit for a fast getaway. She had been at the point of deciding to cancel her student loans when an older professor rose to talk and described an education quite different from that portrayed by the earlier speakers. Instead of lauding information, he outlined the still vibrant world of librarianship, a field he described as separate from information science. After recounting the library career possibilities available both nationally and regionally, this senior professor concluded his remarks by stressing to the "potential librarians" in the audience that the program they had joined did have the necessary courses for their education, although many of them would have to be taken with part-time faculty. A relevant library education, he emphasized was still possible at his institution.

Providentially, there was a happy ending to this visitor's story. She had followed the older professor's advice, avoided the full-time faculty information advocates wherever possible, and enrolled in the courses taught by the part-time instructors with full-time library day jobs. She was also able to secure a librarian position after earning her degree. Following the recounting of her story this newly minted librarian realized she was running late and hurriedly left this writer's office to claim a table and wait for her friend in Dominican University's popular Cyber Café.

Some Implications of the Visitor's Story

After the departure of the unexpected visitor, the author found himself pondering just how many ALA-accredited degree programs could be accused with justification of perpetrating a variety of academic deception in proclaiming that their information education was an adequate schooling for the American and Canadian library worlds.

Was it indeed the case that the preparation of future librarians in ALA-accredited programs was (1) being ignored or minimized by the current generation of information educators, and (2) sustained only through a tenuous alliance of the few new professors who had avoided the effects of "information education" indoctrination, aging "library" faculty pondering just giving up the fight and retiring, and practitioners willing to teach the realities of their profession to the next generation of librarians for the notoriously low pay offered part-time instructors?

Having researched and written on theory, including a book-length work on the topic (Crowley 1999a, 2000, 2005b), the author was aware that this new librarian's story constitutes a near-textbook example of the distinction between the two "theories of action" found in organizations that was offered by Chris Argyris of Harvard University—*espoused theory* and *theory in use*. For the ALA-accredited programs of Canada and the United States, espoused theory can be defined broadly as the stated beliefs, values, and course descriptions usually found in or on brochures, school bulletins, and institutional Web sites. According to Argyris (1999, 126) the espoused or public theory of how an organization works can and does differ markedly from the second type of "theory of action"—theory in use. In terms of this present study the theory in use of a program accredited by ALA is the actual, as opposed to the claimed, education delivered by the school.

Unlike the espoused and often very public claims published in print or on the Internet by educators—claims which can be rather easily identified and analyzed—the actual theories in use may be more difficult to determine. Not every new student has the "benefit" of being told during orientation that, from the point of view of many of the core faculty, her interest in receiving a "library" education in an "information" program was clearly misguided. Normally, the behavior of faculty and programs offering ALA-accredited degrees is more complicated to analyze. Public pronouncements must be weighed in the light of actual conduct or the analysis of less guarded communications—oral, written, electronic, etc.—that can reveal more of the truth than those originating the messages intend to convey. However, in the tale of the aspiring librarian who nearly left her program on the first day, the majority of the full-time faculty present at the orientation at least had the integrity to state their preference for an information education. What is more problematic was the perception conveyed during her orientation session that even in a program accredited by ALA, the education of librarians—as opposed to information specialists and knowledge managers—had become the responsibility of those on the margins of the organization.

THE CURRENT STATE OF "LIBRARY" EDUCATION

Complications to Understanding

Any consideration of how librarian professionalism may be safeguarded and expanded must address the overlapping worlds of library education and librarian employment. While the state of library education may indeed have reached the point where a former ALA president could term it "a disaster that is in danger of becoming a catastrophe" (Gorman 2000, 67), it is equally true that academic, public, and school library employers cannot escape their share of blame for undermining librarian professionalism.

Programs of library and information studies accredited by ALA have been in the midst of an extended round of attacks by a number of practitioners, journalists, and academics over the perceived lack of relevance of their "information" education to "library" realities (Berry 2006; Cox 2006; Gorman 2004; Mulvaney and O'Connor 2006; Wiegand 2005). Less publicized is the reality that the embrace of an information science/corporate model of the library in ALA-accredited programs (Apostle and Raymond 1997) has inculcated an entire generation of senior managers with a vision that redefines the library as merely an information center to be staffed by the least expensive staff necessary to perform information functions. This adherence to the information science "business model" too often replaces librarian with library assistant positions in an effort to do "more with less" and, in the process, even acquire or maintain high national rankings (Crowley 2003, 2006; Hennen 2006).

The very nature of public controversies, which inevitably accumulate both attacks and defenses, makes the process of determining "truth" immensely complicated. Anyone who has participated in a significant public dispute has learned through oftentimes bitter experience that the resulting posturing and spin control, the efforts to manage and define the controversy, can and do make "truth" a contested thing. Through hard experience the social sciences have developed approaches that enhance prospects for determining what is "real" in organizational lives. In a manual written to guide new researchers, the knowledgeable sociologist Howard S. Becker recommended adopting a mindset recognizing that the people who run organizations "always lie a little bit, smoothing over rough spots, hiding troubles, denying the existence of problems" since "what they say may be true, but social organization gives them reasons to lie" (1998, 91). For Becker the primary way to address the statements offered by organizational leaders was to—*"doubt everything anyone in power tells you"* because "a well-socialized participant in society may believe them, but a well-socialized social scientist will suspect the worst and look for it" (1998, 91; emphasis in original).

Although Becker's admonition to consistently doubt has its uses it is, at best, a negative virtue. One simply cannot reject as sources of information all those in power in organizations. The reality of mixed motivations is also in play; people can do things with negative consequences out of what others may see as the best or worst of intentions. However, the likelihood of receiving biased information is often related to whether or not the organizational source is under attack and will benefit from having such information believed. In an effort to secure more trustworthy data this work, wherever possible, will draw on information and knowledge not generated as part of the library versus information argument. There is, for example, considerable value in the analysis of communications by information or library proponents to "friendly" audiences in journals or conference proceedings, as well as in the judgments of political leaders recorded in legislative hearings or other "neutral" venues. Although such resources have differing levels of credibility they are likely to be the best available touchstones against which investigators close can measure the "truths" contained in the manifestos or other passionate communications produced in the often bitter exchanges over the future of librarianship in programs devoted to information education.

Although an attempt will be made in these pages to avoid personal attacks wherever possible, the simple process of participating in controversies can sensitize educators and librarians alike to view any criticism as, at best, unwarranted discourtesy. Nevertheless, at a time when the future of an entire profession may well be at stake, an occasional perceived incivility may be the unavoidable price to be paid to get closer to the realities underlying contested truths.

Warning Signals from the United Kingdom

Space considerations prevent anything like a detailed review of issues affecting the longevity and revitalization of professional librarianship beyond the Canadian and American borders. Nonetheless, it is
worth stressing that the recent history of overseas library education,
particularly that of the United Kingdom forms a disturbing caution-
ary tale for North America's librarian communities. At a minimum the
British experience, although not providing precise analogies for library contexts across the Atlantic, is nevertheless instructive regarding what can happen when a nation's librarians embrace information rhetoric and delay too long the necessary fight to retain an
appropriate library education. The result, in the United Kingdom at
least, is a situation where the professional preparation of librarians is
increasingly being separated from the degrees offered by that nation's
information-centric university world.

Specifically, a number of disquieting developments have worked to
lower twenty-first-century library professionalism in the United
Kingdom. These include

- *Disappearance of preparation for children's librarianship in professional education at the university level* (McGarry 2000, 112). At a
  minimum, this demonstrates an undermining by U.K. higher
  education of the valuable educational work of youth librarians
  in helping to prepare the next generation of that nation's citizens and library users, a service long valued by adult patrons or
  customers of the public library. Furthermore, expelling youth
  services librarianship from the United Kingdom's academic
  world seems to be the leading edge of a development that is
  returning public librarian preparation back to something like
  the millennium-old system of guilds, the basis for educating
  professionals before the rise of the medieval university (below);
- *Testimony presented by the Chartered Institute of Library and
  Information Professionals (CILIP)—roughly the UK's equivalent of
  both ALA and the Special Libraries Association—submitted for the extended hearings on the public library held by the Culture, Media and
  Sport Committee of the House of Commons.* In its formal submission CILIP stressed that "it is a matter of concern that many of
  the courses of professional education in the UK no longer

offer a public library option and most students do not opt for a career in public libraries" (Great Britain 2005, Ev 30). The memorandum, not unexpectedly, noted the appeal of higher salaries for information professionals in the private sector. However, a compounding factor may also be present, a variant of what the sociologist Benjamin Singer termed "availability bias" (1996, 212). In the U.K. context, the choice of student to enter the corporate sector may result, in part, from not being sufficiently exposed to the full spectrum of possibilities inherent in the public library world during her or his university education. Although such work is frequently less financially rewarding it may well be more satisfying for those with an interest in societal betterment;

- *The University of Wales, Banger, official proposal "to sack the majority of its professional librarians in order to save money, on the grounds that they were surplus to requirements in the Internet age"* (Broady-Preston 2006, 52). This proposal, deemed reflective of a contemporary trend in universities, specifically noted that searching databases has moved from a skilled task to something requiring far less than a librarian qualification.

The Canary in the Library Education "Coal Mine"

For many decades miners went down to the coal pits accompanied for safety reasons by canaries, birds that were known to be particularly sensitive to the often-lethal gasses generated by the mining process. Consequently, any sign of their physical distress was treated as warning that the miners were in danger and needed to take immediate action to survive. As will be discussed more in Chapter 4, the ongoing abandonment of relevant librarian education by British universities, and the consequent necessity of public librarians to retreat into guild-like training, has become the proverbial canary in the mine shaft for North American professional education and practice. It is a warning to Canadian and American librarians and sympathetic educators of the urgent necessity to reform their university programs and, in the process, develop appropriate, noninformation courses and theories to support librarian professionalism within the academic, public, and school library sectors.

CONTEMPORARY NORTH AMERICAN
"LIBRARY" EDUCATION

Writing in 1997, the Canadian library and information educator Boris Raymond succinctly summarized the problem being faced by contemporary librarians and librarians-to-be who are seeking a relevant professional education: Educators have implemented an "information paradigm" for the library and information studies field that asserts "since everything that libraries handle is 'information,' 'library' and 'information' work are one and the same thing" (Raymond 1997, 7–8). When Raymond and his coauthor Richard Apostle analyzed this reduction of librarianship to one of its parts in *Librarianship and the Information Paradigm,* they repeatedly found how inappropriate the for-profit information model was for the vast spectrum of library activities (1997). In the process they also revealed how seeing academic, public, and school libraries as predominately information providers obscures the fundamental differences relating to the needs of their users that separate information services from library services (Raymond 1997, 16).

Subsequent to the work of Apostle and Raymond, Marcia J. Bates, one of North America's leading information theorists, offered what has become an influential rationale for subsuming "library" under "information" when she argued for the existence of "meta-disciplines" such as "information science, education and journalism" related to the transmission of knowledge across "content disciplines," presumably including the dozens of other academic fields that also have an interest in information. In her theorizing Bates connected

- *information science* with the "storage and retrieval" of knowledge,
- *education* with its "teaching and learning," and
- *journalism* with the "discovery and transmission of news" (1999, 1044).

Upon analysis it can be seen that Bates was correct in several particulars but was fundamentally wrong in her conception of libraries. She was largely right about the realities of corporate and research information and knowledge management centers, entities staffed by those who can see the immediate applicability of information science to their operations. However, the education meta-discipline is much more appropriate for describing the realities of academic, public, and school libraries. Indeed, the identification of academic, public, and school libraries with education and learning has become even more acute with the growing realization that the traditional library triad of education-information-recreation has become something of a dyad, with the preponderance of what had been seen as the library's recreational functions, specifically including spare time reading, now seen as having a fundamentally educational component (Ross, McKechnie, and Rothbauer 2006).

The Impact of The Information Science Business Model on Library Practice

A critical problem with a professional library education dominated by an information science model permeated with the values of the profit-making sector is that it provides little or no justification for defending the inherent worth of librarian professionalism. In a prescient 1995 article titled "Do 'We' Have a Future?" Bill Whitson, then-president of the California Academic & Research Libraries, identified the following factors impacting professional academic librarians, including the adoption by higher education of what he termed "the 'commercial' ethos" wherein

- respect is accorded only to the ability to "do the job at hand";
- technology has devalued the expertise that librarians accumulated in a print environment;
- market emphasis on present effectiveness and an immediately relevant skill set is prized over a history of prior achievements;
- "flexibility, imagination and the ability to learn quickly" are valued over "tenure, degrees, credentials and job 'classifications,'" and such long-established qualifications are now seen as roadblocks to organizational effectiveness;
- academic decision makers, specifically including faculty, are willing to pay for library resources, not professional librarians (Whitson 1995).

For Whitson, the business model's emphasis on present skills and the devaluation of "credentials" and "degrees," "job classifications," and other evidence of established academic expertise, undermines both higher education's support for the ALA-accredited master's degree and the award of academic status for "all those involved in original cataloging, reference, administration, or even collection development" (1995). It is of interest that Whitson's proposed response to the problems outlined, that academic librarians ought to accept their downward spiral of a future as information professionals and endure relentless job re-structuring, represents an attitude of resignation verging on defeat-ism that underscores the essentially negative implications for librar-ian professionalism of embracing Bates's information model (1999).

The concept of librarian as information provider is an intellectual formulation that can lead one to ignore the more positive implica-tions of conceptualizing the librarian as a facilitator of education and lifelong learning. Learning, or the potential for learning, exists through-out the life span of a healthy human being and a vibrant human soci-ety. Competing as one of many potential information intermediaries at a time when a do-it-yourself approach is on the rise is likely to make librarianship a case study for a class on occupational irrelevance. A session or two in an online or on-site MPA or MBA course devoted to the librarian's professional suicide through adoption of the informa-tion model at the very time when information self-service came into fashion may even replace long-standing discussions of the irrelevance of buggy whip manufacturers after the arrival of automobiles or how railroads got it wrong when they operated on the model that they were in the railroad instead of the transportation business.

THE SHORTAGE OF LIBRARY THEORY

Any effort to provide a theoretical basis for sustaining or returning to professional librarian education must address the problem identi-fied by John M. Budd when he examined available theories on the mat-ter of "relevance" in matching answers to questions (Budd 2004). In his review of the in-print research, Budd observed that recent theoriz-ing and modeling in this area tends to be dominated by the "informa-tion" wing of what ALA terms "library and information studies." Relevant theoretical publications by library theorists, writers who be-lieve that information theory and models do not comprehend all that libraries do, are largely absent from the literature of the transitional field known as library and information studies.

A consideration of the reasons why library-oriented professors teaching in ALA-accredited programs were not theorizing from a "library" perspective appeared, somewhat ironically, in the fiftieth an-niversary issue of one of the core journals of information science. This essay addressed such realities as the

1. prevalence among information theorists and educators of "mythic fact"—defined as a claim asserted without adequate

proof and involving both fact and fiction—that everything libraries do can be explained by information theory;

2. socialization of new doctoral students, possible future "library" educators, into an information ideology that causes them to look at their professional world through an information, not a library, lens;

3. fashion ascendant in the field, with "information" being in fashion and "library" being out of fashion;

4. perception that manuscripts written from an information perspective are more likely to be published in prestigious journals or with preferred publishers than manuscripts taking a library point of view—a critically important factor in the not-always-successful grind to earn tenure and promotion;

5. reality that library practitioners tend to distrust theory, even library theory, so the only possible audience for such theory tends to be the same faculty who have already declared an allegiance to the information concept of the library (Crowley 1999b).

Simply stated, under the current system of "library" education supposedly monitored for quality control by ALA as part of "library and information studies," the culture of programs accredited by ALA, the rewards system of the parent institution, and a history of a practitioner negativity toward faculty research, strongly discourage anyone from developing library theory. The failure of ALA and the influence of academic culture will be addressed further in Chapters 3 and 4. At this point is useful to devote a few words to explaining why library professionals are often resistant to theories developed at the university level.

THE DISCONNECTION BETWEEN FACULTY THEORY AND PROFESSIONAL PRACTICE

"But There Have Always Been Complaints About Library Education"

A standard response by some educators to accusations that information-dominated ALA-accredited programs do not provide an appropriate professional library education and are not developing useful library theory is the appeal to history—the "but there have always been complaints about library education" argument. Writing in

1985, Samuel Rothstein of the University of British Columbia's ALA-accredited program even offered "An Anthology of Abuse: 97 Years of Criticism of Library Schools" that was published as part of his *Library Journal* article titled "Why People Really Hate Library Schools" (42–43). Rothstein's conclusion was to put the blame for the perceived problem of educational and research irrelevance on the complaining librarians, terming them "querulous loners" who "don't fit in with a group," and who seemingly had entered the profession of librarianship to escape stress and were resentful of the pressure they encounter in their professional work (1985, 47–48). Simply summarized, the article is a near-perfect example of a "blame the victim" approach designed to deflect responsibility from those most responsible for program irrelevance—the faculty in Canadian and American ALA-accredited programs.

It is a useful exercise in humility for educators to recall that there is a long record of perceived irrelevance in the education of professional librarians. However, in the 1887–1985 period, this disconnection was often mitigated through a shared library culture, reinforced by the ability of experienced professional librarians with master's degrees to become full-time teachers and mentors of future librarians without interrupting their careers to earn a Ph.D. The possibilities for such mitigation across the faculty-practitioner divide have become significantly more limited as the information culture embraced by so many faculty and the library culture lived by academic, public, and school professionals have increasingly diverged.

From the perspective of cultural pragmatism, variations of the "they never liked us anyway" argument represent a poor defense against the accumulating evidence demonstrating that the information instruction of ALA-accredited programs in recent decades has often left their graduates ill-equipped to help solve fundamentally important societal problems involving reading and lifelong education. If professional instruction is increasingly irrelevant to the education needed by twenty-first-century practitioners to address the library priorities of American and Canadian publics and governments, the present fault lies much more with the information educators of 2007 than with their predecessor library educators of 1887 or 1967.

Resistance to Faculty-Generated Theory

On several occasions the author has addressed the issue of why library and information practitioners avoid using faculty-generated theory even when such theory appears to be relevant. Briefly stated, such reasons cluster around the (1) variation in the consequences for researchers and practitioners if such theory proves to be erroneous; and (2) reliance by practitioners on the experience of other professionals who have successfully addressed the same or related problem (Crowley 1999a, 285–286).

Variations in Consequences for Using Erroneous Theory

Simply stated, "library" and "information" researchers suffer far less from the consequences of "theory failure" than the practitioners who make the mistake of allocating scarce resources as the basis of such theory since

> "Information" and "library" educators exist within complex academic environments where the rules and reward systems are vastly different from the worlds of practice. In the research university, for example, articles written by a faculty member on the basis of an erroneous theory can simply result in other professors writing articles in opposition. The faculty member under attack may even see the resulting citations as positive. Disputes conduced in the "literature" of a field or discipline tend to increase the "citation count" or the references to an author's body of work. Such citations can assume a critical importance in promotion and tenure decisions. Alternately, in the world of practice, allocating scarce resources on the basis of that professor's erroneous theory might cost the job of a library or information center head. (Crowley 1999b, 1131)

To state the matter in the bluntest possible terms, faculty theory need not have any discernible connection with library and information realities to be of benefit to the careers of academic researchers. For practitioners involved in action that could be influenced by faculty-generated theory, the necessity for such theory to be "right" rises to the level of an imperative since jobs may be on the line.

Practitioner Guidance for Solving Library Problems

Successful library and information managers tend to follow a predicable pattern—almost a line-by-line script—in the planning necessary to alter the operation of their organizations. First, when the need for a new or altered service is discerned, managers consult their own experience. If that proves insufficient, they consider the expertise available elsewhere in the organization, in their professional and personal networks, the possibilities offered by the practitioner or management literature, and/or the knowledge of similar challenges residing with consultants with a demonstrable track record of success. They tend not to consult the theoretical works of library and information professors because experience (their own or that of other practitioners) has shown them that it is preferable to identify related organizations of comparable size where similar, if not identical challenges, have been mastered. It is not unknown, for example, for library and information managers involved in designing a new building or offering a new or enhanced service to travel widely to visit possible exemplars, nearly always spending time with those involved in their management and delivery, asking both initial and follow-up questions and deriving guidance from both the answers and the contexts in which the answers were delivered. It is a process involving the identification of explicit information and the surfacing of tacit or less public knowledge, knowledge whose sharing is often signaled by such observations as

- "There wasn't a whole lot of data, but I had a gut feeling how this would work."
- "Now that you ask, we actually did it this way. Let me talk you through it."
- "I'll deny it if you quote me, but this is my thinking on how we really solved that problem."
- "Forget what the newspapers and Web logs reported, this is what really happened and why."

Although accounts of failures tend not to appear in the library and information practitioner literature and stories of successes usually follow the rule that organizations and their managers obscure the embarrassing and highlight the positive, they represent an underutilized and extremely promising gateway to the development of useful library and information theory (Crowley 2005b).

Research Relevance and the Perspective of the Congressional Research Service

In a recent monograph titled *Spanning the Theory-Practice Divide in Library and Information Science* (2005b), the author explored in depth a range of factors that cumulatively work to make faculty research irrelevant for practitioners within the many arenas addressed by library and information studies. Briefly summarized, such factors reflect a cultural divide that has only deepened through the employment of faculty lacking substantial experience in libraries and information organizations. As with their counterparts in other professions, disciplines, and fields, library and information professors often do not wish to accept the reality that the cultures of off-campus practitioners, which judge research largely on the basis of its usefulness in solving problems, and the cultures of faculty researchers, which often prize research elegance at expense of "real-world" applicability, simply operate on the basis of radically different norms (Crowley 2005b).

In consequence, demands that practitioners must somehow be socialized to embrace faculty norms for judging research (research elegance) at the expense of community or organizational mores (research effectiveness in solving critical problems) often appear absurd to working professionals and are likely to be ignored. This result is particularly so when practitioners can secure assistance from consultants who understand that demonstrating present problem-solving effectiveness is often a prerequisite for obtaining future consulting contracts (Crowley 2005b, 169–178).

The Congressional Research Service (CRS) is the nonpartisan and highly valued research arm of the Library of Congress that produces a broad spectrum of analyses and evaluations for the members, committees, and staff of the U.S. Senate and House of Representatives. Such research is regularly undertaken in areas ranging from disputes with the executive branch (presidency) over policy at the international level to focused considerations of issues more relevant to a given congressional district or state. In 1986 the CRS addressed in depth the issue of research effectiveness in a now-classic report commissioned by the Task Force on Science Policy of the House Committee on Science and Technology, a document eventually issued as *Research Policies for the Social and Behavioral Sciences* (Library of Congress 1986). In disseminating this report as an official document, the House committee endorsed the CRS findings that

> It may be that some expectations for using behavioral and social science research directly in policymaking do not recognize the many obstacles both to the production of policy-relevant knowledge and also to its application in complex processes of bureaucratic and political decisionmaking. Some of the obstacles that affect researchers

are discussed in this report. They include: producing counterintuitive findings, producing research which is irrelevant to policymaking, political naiveté regarding bureaucratic functioning and the vagaries of political decisionmaking, conflicts stemming from the need to respond to the academic reward system which may differ from the rewards of policy-advising, inadequate knowledge and inappropriate quantification, and fraud and deception. (Library of Congress 1986, 4)

Library and information research frequently relies on the same social science theories that CRS identified as so often unproductive in solving problems in the off-campus world. The daily environments of most practitioner communities simply do not work according to the limited variable and controlled environment models advanced by faculty theorists. In consequence, it is quite understandable that the majority of library practitioners, who are employed outside of higher education environments, and even academic librarians on university and college campuses, might see as incomprehensible the continuing demands of the research and teaching faculty that they rely on faculty research when designing library programs and services.

The True Value of Research in the "Real" World

Most libraries and information centers are parts of local or other government entities and share their parent organization's operational culture. It is likely that a similar reality is in play for those libraries, information, and knowledge centers that are components of private-sector organizations. In making decisions, the CRS study found that government entities take into account a range of inputs, many unquantifiable, including "values, advocacy or interest group pressures, and scientific information—to name but a few." In the real but very messy world of organizational decision making, "scientific" studies play minor roles. Instead, the "validity of behavioral and social science information is measured against standards embodied in the consensus of prevailing social and political values. Verified, or even non-verified, behavioral and social information will be used in policymaking if it coincides with these values" (Library of Congress 1986, 221).

Information educators who consider librarians and library-minded educators to be overly concerned with values should keep in mind that such values are usually the basis for action in many professional worlds, specifically including librarianship. These environments, the settings for action that often cannot be captured by any study that ignores difficult to quantify aspects of reality, are sometimes known only on a tacit level and then only by those able to understand the reality that is so often hidden by easily measured variables (Crowley 2005b).

In its analysis of the value of research to decision making by government units, the CRS discerned that "studies of knowledge utilization" have determined that it is virtually impossible to connect a given piece of research with adoption of a specific organizational policy. Furthermore, the researchers opined that the most valuable social science research, over a period of years, serves to "enlighten" "an opinion maker, ordinary concerned citizen, or a decisionmaker" and that it is best not to expect the equation of a given piece of research with a "specific decisionmaking sequence" (Library of Congress 1986, 176). The cause and effect of research is usually impossible to prove.

The research examined in the author's recent work on theory development (Crowley 2005b) and the focused analysis of the CRS (Library of Congress 1986), repeatedly demonstrate that studies based on meeting academic norms so vital to promotion and tenure are inapplicable to off-campus, problem-solving contexts in the vast majority of circumstances. The fact that such research is yet produced reflects the undeniable reality that the faculty rewards system of higher education, through institutional promotion and tenure processes, supports its development, regardless of its relevance to off-campus environments.

Research and New Academic Librarians

As library practitioners working in higher education contexts, academic librarians on the tenure track are often at a disadvantage in meeting university and college standards for research and publication. In four-year colleges and universities, the reality is that most of the research and classroom faculty have earned a Ph.D. or other doctorate and have received substantial training in conducting academically acceptable research. It is often the case that the initial publications of new faculty reflect the scholarship embodied in their doctoral studies. Since most academic librarians lack a doctorate and are likely to have received their ALA-accredited master's degrees from programs where a thesis is not required, registering for the courses supporting master's degree research or scholarship was seldom a priority in their studies. In consequence, a pragmatic argument can be made that academic librarians lacking a thesis as a component of their ALA-accredited degree, particularly if they do not have a master's degree in another field, are at a competitive disadvantage when judged by the same tenure and promotion standards that apply to Ph.D.-holding faculty.

In Chapter 6, a recommended process for devising courses necessary for appropriate library and information educations will be explored. For their own benefit, academic librarians participating in this proposed examination may want to examine the worth of ALA encouraging a thesis option in accredited master's degree programs, if only for the practical reason of jump starting the research and publication needed for tenure by librarians in many higher education communities.

If the now-classic yet still relevant cautions regarding research irrelevance offered by the CRS regarding research relevance are a significant component of discussions regarding the possibility of encouraging students to take research methods courses, and if educators abandon their long-standing demand that off-campus librarians and information specialists adopt higher education's norms for judging research, it is possible that requiring a research course in the education of all librarians and information specialists could contribute to the ability of libraries to solve pressing societal problems. Many practitioners are intuitive pragmatists and possess mindsets that tend to respond favorably to proven methods of addressing pressing difficulties that have been implemented by their peers. Unfortunately, to date, educators have delivered relatively little in the way of such assistance.

Successful "Library" Theory

Although it remains true that information research dominates in library and information studies, there are worthy exceptions to this rule. A few library-influenced monographs, comprising sustained efforts at theory development, have either been written or compiled and include John E. Buschman's *Dismantling the Public Sphere: Situating and Sustaining Librarianship in the Age of the New Public Philosophy* (2003), Ronald B. McCabe's *Civic Librarianship: Renewing the Social Mission of the Public Library* (2001), and Thomas Augst and Wayne Wiegand's multi-authored *The Library as an Agency of Culture* (2001). In addition, Wiegand's numerous individual chapters and articles (2001, 2003) and even Michael Gorman's heartfelt jeremiads (2000, 2004) reflect fundamentally sound critiques of those redefining important library concerns as not worthy of extended study within the increasingly information-centric worlds of ALA-accredited programs.

For pragmatic reasons to be discussed later in this work, "social mission," "public sphere," and, somewhat paradoxically, even the massive intellectual concept termed "culture" are unlikely to be effective in serving as an organizing principle for assembling the critical mass of practitioners and public policy makers necessary at national, state, and local levels necessary to draw the interest of entrepreneurial ALA-accredited programs in a library direction. In addition, they might be too little understood within the library community or insufficiently acceptable within the university to function as viable alternatives to the library as component of the information vision advocated by many theorists. Social mission, public sphere, and cultural approaches can and do offer productive insights relevant to library realities, but in the struggle for the survival of the professional librarian the vision that currently best meets the criteria of significance, sustainability, and direction in North American contexts is the historic education model, updated as the "learning model of the library" to better reflect present understandings.

Theory and Library Models

One aim of this publication is to stimulate theorizing within library science–librarianship through providing "library-friendly faculty" with some of the concepts necessary to undertake the required studies on which to write future introductory texts for a field substantially different from information science. Through (1) exploring the historic and emerging components of the model of the librarian and library as learning facilitators, particularly as worked out in lifecycle librarianship, and (2) by concentrating on examining what academic, public, and school librarians actually do in and out of libraries, this work also demonstrates the significant limitations in the information model. It is undeniable that librarians' professional responsibilities in academic, public, and school environments include some information-related duties. Yet in some contexts, the information provision efforts of academic, public, and school libraries constitutes a nonmathematical lowest common denominator. Information is delivered, but it is not the primary purpose of the enterprise, certainly not at the fundamentally important intermediary roles played by information specialists, knowledge managers, and competitive data analysts in the corporate and research sectors. Most libraries, particularly in the public sector, are learning facilitators, both in law and in fact. It is their primary purpose; they do not exist as information agencies which happen to support learning as a byproduct of a fundamental information purpose.

A Fresh Lens on The Library's Educational/Learning Roles

In her consideration of the critical formative years of the American public library titled *Apostles of Culture: The Public Librarian and American Society, 1876–1920,* the Canadian academic Dee Garrison explored how public librarians could regularly publish "denunciations of 'immoral literature'"—usually fiction, hence the seemingly perennial "fiction problem"—while purchasing "in abundance" the very same works they were protesting (1979, 61). She found that the combination of book protest and popular fiction lending constituted a sort of professional ritual where librarian ideals about the need for people to read uplifting works confronted the reality that the library could not force "the poor and the workingmen . . . to make use of its offerings" (1979, 62). If the public library wanted a clientele, its librarians and other staff had to provide the type of reading that the reading public preferred.

It has been the better part of a century since the 1920 concluding date of the period of Garrison's study. These early librarians simply did not have access to an accumulating body of research demonstrating that simple "reading volume"—the quantity, not the quality of reading—makes "a significant contribution to multiple measures of vocabulary, general knowledge, spelling and verbal fluency" even at the level of college students (Cunningham and Stanovich 1998, 5). Nevertheless, allowing for such other motivations as insuring a regular stream of "customers," these public librarians could not but notice the effects of reading on borrowers, regardless of what they read, and undoubtedly knew that there was value in what they were doing. They simply lacked the vocabulary to describe how culturally condemned reading material could somehow help advance progress toward the socially desirable goal of a reading populace. In their professional education these early librarians had not been taught to trust their own experience and prize what today's researchers often term professional tacit knowledge, defined as the "often-undocumented wisdom possessed by expert practitioners" (Crowley 1999a, 282).

Librarians practicing in the decades immediately before and after 1900 simply lacked the mental models necessary to understand that their willingness to provide popular material to encourage both reading and use of the public library, their experience-based decision to deliver a service useful to their communities, was not a failing to be ignored or denied. Rather, acquiring material appropriate to a range of patrons, users, or customers, including those who in the twenty-first century might be termed "new readers," demonstrated their admirable ability "to adapt to, select, and shape environments in order to solve everyday problems" (Matthew, Cianciolo, and Sternberg 2005, 6). A significant number of the librarians serving from 1876 to 1920 somehow understood but lacked the terminology to articulate what is only now becoming an increasingly common knowledge. Since their time decades of research on reading have demonstrated

- men, women, and children become readers by doing "lots of reading of extended text";
- "novice readers" are stimulated by the sheer pleasure of reading;
- academic, public, and school libraries need to support reading for pleasure by
  - making available the books people actually want to read;
  - demonstrating the value of a love of reading; and
  - creating "face-to-face" or online "communities of readers" (Ross, McKechnie, and Rothbauer 2006, ix).

Understanding of the learning roles of public libraries is not limited to comprehending their commitment to developing readers. These roles will be discussed in some depth in Chapter 6. For the present, it is enough to note that children's programming in such libraries continues to maintain its educational intent, while sessions for teens have embraced active—and enjoyable—learning. A similar development has affected the services offered adults. During the spring 2007 semester, a senior library manager serving as a guest presenter in the author's

graduate course on public library issues described how adult programming had evolved in the last ten to fifteen years in suburban Chicago
public libraries. In the past such programming frequently could be
termed "Chamber of Commerce style" since it usually consisted of sessions on such limited topics as estate planning, insurance needs, and
financial instruments delivered by community businesses with a
Chamber of Commerce membership and the mixed motivation of
helping the community while promoting their products. Throughout
the Chicago suburbs—and most particularly in the presenter's own library—such activity has evolved into "community programming." As
such it can embrace sessions on a variety of local, national, and international issues, including, in one library, no fewer than five groups
regularly meeting to discuss the problems of the Middle East; sessions
on new exhibits in the library art gallery, theatrical or music programs,
film viewings and discussions, book discussions, etc. (James Madigan,
presentation to class, February 7, 2007).

It is often the case that preparation for the role of a librarian as facilitator in a community learning center is not sufficiently addressed
in ALA-accredited programs except in courses dedicated to youth services. This is particularly unfortunate since public librarians now increasingly understand, as previously observed, that the former trio of
library services—education, information, and recreation—has now
been transformed into a duo—learning (education) and information.
Under the right circumstances it is possible to be both entertaining
and informative, yet too many librarians have earned their ALA-
accredited degrees without gaining an understanding of how best to
achieve such a positive outcome in a variety of library environments.
To justify public support for twenty-first-century libraries, and in particular for the professionalism of librarians employed in such contexts, it will be necessary to move beyond the prevailing information
rhetoric to provide a more appropriate intellectual lens for viewing
the services and programs they plan and deliver, and for securing
the education most appropriate to the next generation of library
practitioners.

RESPONDING TO IRRELEVANT PROFESSIONAL EDUCATION

The misapplication of information education to library contexts actually supports the arguments of cost-cutters who see the salaries of

professional librarians as an unnecessary expense at a time when the library as business model argues for substituting less prepared and lower compensated human alternatives. In consequence, it makes little sense for professional librarians to utilize information models that undermine their own relevance. ALA-accredited education is clearly in need of reform, yet the revitalization effort cannot be based on outraged rhetoric (Gorman 2000). It will require more than slogans. America's national and state academic, public, and school library communities will need to put aside inappropriate information concepts and employ library understandings to comprehend why they are valued by their users, patrons, and customers. They will then need to use such understandings in first-level negotiations with information educators who may well be willing to satisfy both library and information professional needs through appropriate courses and degrees. At worst, should negotiations fail at this stage, comprehension of the real reasons libraries and librarians are valued will provide the necessary components of the agendas for discussing relevant library education at the higher levels of

- university provosts, presidents, and boards of trustees;
- state boards of higher education or other coordinating bodies;
- state legislatures.

Securing appropriate library education from all programs accredited by ALA is going to take time and involve agreement on what constitutes a relevant education before campaigning to receive it. It is a practical demand of sympathetic educators that deserves to be heeded. At times, a unified library community with an agenda for educational reform may encounter information faculty, including deans with no library experience and little in the way of shared memories with a library constituency, who honestly believe that information theory trumps learning from practitioner experience in designing appropriate library education. Under such circumstances, even in university contexts notoriously resistant to demands by outside constituencies, responsiveness may still be possible. At worst, it will require that same unified library community, whose advocacy efforts have always been based on politically active public librarians, trustees, and friends, remember that it truly is the proverbial sleeping tiger that, when roused to fight for its survival, is capable of achieving educational and political goals at the most senior policy levels, up to and including organizing to defeat a powerful Speaker of the House on a vote in his own chamber (Crowley 1994). With luck and mutual goodwill, disagreements over an appropriate education between communities of library practitioners and alliances of faculty and administrators involved with or in ALA-accredited programs can be settled far short of a meeting of a university board of trustees or a legislative committee. This is particularly so in the cases of state-assisted universities and their entrepreneurial private counterparts.

At this point, both supporters of appropriate library education and skeptical information educators might reasonably ask why the current pattern of offering an information education that privileges running the library like the proverbial business can be so toxic to librarian professionalism. To provide the necessary background it is useful to look at how the information science–supported business philosophy of the library has become a caustic acid for librarianship.

Striking A Nerve

It the April 15, 2003, issue of *Library Journal* the author published "The Suicide of the Public Librarian," an article detailing some of the negative consequences for librarian professionalism resulting from employers following information science's "best practices" and running the public library as a for-profit business clone, specifically as a low-cost purveyor of information (Crowley 2003). For the author, the preferred approach, offering a better opportunity for preserving the careers of professional librarians, was to envision the public library in a library science mode. That meant seeing the library as a community learning resource requiring well-educated professionals who, at times, provide information and do so effectively.

This article drew a substantial range of support and criticism (John N. Berry III, personal communication June 2006). Since the work employed certain theoretical formulations, the author was able to use it as a case study of how to popularize theory in the subsequent *Spanning the Theory-Practice Divide in Library and Information Science* (Crowley 2005b). However, due to the nature of that work and publisher's deadlines, it was not possible to discuss the strong responses "from the field" to the 2003 article nor analyze in print the similarly intense pro and con reactions to follow-up essays published as "Save Professionalism" in the September 1, 2005, issue of *Library Journal* (Crowley 2005a; John N. Berry III, personal communication, June 2006) and as "Suicide

Prevention" in the spring 2006 issue of *Library Administration & Management* (Crowley 2006). Since the present work is concerned with renewing professional librarianship, it provides the author with the opportunity to remedy such omissions in discussing the future of libraries and librarians.

The business model of the library, long supported by information science, tends to dismiss librarian professional concerns and values as either irrelevant or an impediment to effective library service (Cronin 1995, 897; Deane 2003). For "librarian as information provider" adherents utilizing the business model of libraries involves a focus on the costs of delivering the same "information product" that the business world now assumes to be more or less a standardized commodity (Corcoran, Dagar, and Stratigos 2000). Here it should be noted recognizing that information is indeed a commodity that does not require seeing its collection, organization, delivery, and use—all valid information science concerns—as the primary component of librarianship.

Central to the critique of the business model of the library in the 2003 *Library Journal* article "Suicide of the Public Librarian" was an examination of how a nationally recognized public library, euphemistically termed the "Jonestown Public Library," was helping to maintain its preeminent status by ruthlessly deprofessionalizing its librarians. The article had its genesis in the stories provided by both former students of the author and other members of his professional network. Such stories were acquired during and a twenty-three-year career working in public and state libraries, as well as a multitype library cooperative, in New York, Alabama, Indiana, and Ohio before the author studied full-time for his Ph.D. These anecdotes represented accounts of how professional librarian positions were being downgraded in public, academic, and school environments. Taken together such stories outlined a relentless commitment to short-term expediency where library directors and boards, school principals, and university provosts saw librarians as overpriced intermediaries in the information life cycle, subject to replacement by less costly alternatives for information provision. In the world of the "Jonestown Public Library," such cost containment involved

- repeatedly reducing librarian positions to the levels of library associate or library assistant;
- systematically underpaying professional librarians whose life circumstances made them unlikely to move on;

- taking all collection development responsibilities away from public service librarians and assigning such responsibilities to part-time librarian selectors; and
- thoughtlessly taking storytelling responsibilities away from youth services librarians.

On the "how to do it right side," in the "Suicide" article the author provided the example of Anthony W. Miele, a former director of the Alabama Public Library Service, who fought doubters and bean counters alike to make the support of librarian professionalism a keystone of his very successful career as a library leader. Miele clashed with state government analysts and other department heads over position descriptions and salary ranges to insure that professional librarians received the recognition and compensation earned by their valuable work.

When the April 15, 2003, issue of *LJ* appeared, "Suicide of the Public Librarian" became a topic of lunchtime conversations among library administrators, librarians, and support staff. From the accounts received by the author it was learned that senior administrators often fumed over or dismissed the article's proposals to delay or avoid deprofessionalization; front-line librarians frequently embraced the arguments; and support staff wondered what was in it for them. There were, of course, the usual contradictory letters to the editor (Letters 2003). Conversely, the responses that were less public proved to be the most revealing. The author learned that then *LJ* Editor-in Chief John N. Berry III was using the article in the regular seminar on professional writing he taught for Dominican University in the summer of 2003. This was in part because Berry saw that the piece had generated a substantial number of negative emails and other communications from the administrators of the public libraries that were so highly ranked by Thomas J. Hennen Jr. and his Hennen's American Public Library Ratings (HAPLR) ratings. By tacit agreement the author did not ask for and Berry did not reveal the identities of the libraries and directors involved.

For the most part, "The Suicide of the Public Librarian" brought the author a very different type of communication, one that showing the cost to library morale of following the corporate business model that seems a fundamental component of information science (Apostle and Raymond 1997). A number of reflective, frequently poignant, and obviously confidential emails were received from the human victims of deprofessionalization, the demoralized librarians working in public libraries from California to Virginia. Among other comments, these librarians wrote

- "Seems as if you opened a can of worms with your *LJ* article. Good for you ;-)";
- "Wonderful article—absolutely on target. Perhaps JPL [Jonestown Public Library] is elsewhere, but [name of Georgia library] fits the description remarkably";
- "Although you did not mention the library system, it could have been [name of Maryland public library]";
- "Your recent article in LIBRARY JOURNAL is all the rage . . . at [name of California public library]. Perhaps you were really writing about our library system! Every professional insult that you describe is in full bloom here. But we consider it a homicide perpetrated by our administration, rather than a self-inflicted demise";
- "I want to thank you for giving the adult services librarians at [name of Illinois public library] a moment of validation. Two of our librarians discovered the article and quickly made copies for the rest of us, also passing it on to management. The smiles in the Adult Services Workroom have been rare and they were large on that day." (Anonymous email messages to author from April 14, 2003, to July 30, 2003)

On a more positive note, the Chicago Public Library was cited for its commitment to supporting the professional librarian.

So, the reader might ask, why did a long-serving library administrator turned educator attack libraries that were doing nothing more than implementing the business ideas of information science advocated by a generation of consultants and conference presenters? Why criticize practices that were institutionalized by some of the nation's leading public libraries? The answer is simple. These business approaches are incredibly detrimental to the survival of public librarianship as a profession because they reflect

- a critical misreading of fundamentally important American values;
- the pervasiveness of a for-profit, information science management philosophy within the public library community that erroneously privileges the corporate concept of information provider over the historic, more realistic, and better supported role as community center of lifelong learning;

- the inability of many, including public library boards and directors, to comprehend the essentially learning nature of the public library's recreational and informational roles;
- the inherent bias within the business model toward control of the public library by MBA-educated managers, not library directors with professionally relevant educations; and
- the dominance of corporate "information" and "knowledge" principles within programs accredited by ALA.

The adoption by library managers of the business model potentially has long-term and very negative implications for the managers themselves. If the business model is best understood by business graduates, why not hire only MBAs as public library directors, whether or not they possess a degree from an ALA-accredited program? From a business model perspective it makes sense. Students at MBA programs far outnumber the graduates of library and information programs at the graduate level. The August 25, 2006, issue of the *Chronicle of Higher Education* reported that 6,015 "library science" master's degrees and 139,344 "business, management, and marketing" master's degrees were awarded in the 2003–2004 academic year ("Earned Degrees Conferred 2006" 22).

Assuming a normal distribution of intelligence, these figures suggest that there are more or less twenty-three prospective business program managers for every possible library and information program manager educated in a given year. In the MBA business model so supported by information science, managers are presumed to be able to manage anything. A few moments reflection and the negative implications for future librarian leadership in the information science-connected role of *library as business* should be clear. The focus on "business" simply crowds out support for the many valuable educational or learning roles contained in the title "librarian."

Given this reality, savvy administrators have long understood that the corporate/information approach of measuring performance on the basis of *ROI* or *return on investment* is an inadequate basis for calculating library effectiveness. In the academic, public, and school cultures that support libraries demonstrating what the author terms *ROEI* or *return on emotional investment* is almost always a superior strategy for developing and sustaining support. The existence of "Friends of the Library" organizations argues for far more than a relationship based solely on financial return.

Reversing The Slow Death of The Professional "Librarian" and "Librarianship"

The Importance of Effective Communication

It is a truism that words are important, but it is much less emphasized that many efforts to communicate fail when those involved lack common definitions of the matters under discussion (Crowley 2005b). Using quotations marks around the terms "librarian" and "librarianship" recognizes that definitions of a professional librarian and the field of librarianship are contested in the early years of the twenty-first century. A substantial part of this dispute results from the efforts of certain faculty members in the latecomer field variously termed "information," "information science," or "information studies," etc.—presumably with the best of intentions—to advance the claim that library science or librarianship is a "legacy discipline" (Harmon 2006a, 2006b) whose concerns form only a small, subordinate aspect of their own domain.

In talking with the author about what can be termed the "legacy issue," one former student with an extensive career in information technology remarked that in the IT world, "legacy" was professional shorthand for outdated computer systems to be replaced when transition money becomes available and the upgrading can be accomplished without significant impact on the organization, specifically including minimization of any lost income. The author knows a number of information advocates who have a much more supportive view of librarianship, and he has long wondered if the intellectual leaders of the information wing within library and information studies ever seriously considered the negative implications of terming Canadian and American librarianship an intellectual "legacy" rather than recognizing it as a vibrant, growing, and publicly supported solution to a number of pressing societal problems.

On numerous occasions, most recently during site visits to evaluate student practicums and in conversations following the public lectures offered by Dominican University's Graduate School of Library and Information Science, the author has discussed their professional education with new practitioners holding librarian positions within the Chicago metropolitan area. These entry-level professionals reported that in their ALA-accredited programs they were often discouraged from viewing themselves as future librarians by information scholars who wanted them to see their working worlds through the *information lens*, instead the more appropriate and realistic *library lens* that is almost inevitably necessary for success in academic, public, and school environments. The cognitive dissonance or internal mental conflict developing in new librarians as a result of such an inappropriate professional socialization serves to increase the library profession's objections to a system of ALA-accredited education where professors erroneously attempt to apply information solutions to the majority of library problems.

Explorations of the information norms must begin with its debatable assumption that professional librarians are components of the "information infrastructure," a presumption particularly observable in the courses and textbooks used to educate new professionals (Rubin 2004). Both the professors and the texts they use in real or virtual classrooms refuse to concede that librarianship or library studies has the status of a independent, vibrant enterprise, a field regularly encountering and addressing new challenges in a distinctly library context. It is an unfortunate reality that resentment at being classified as a legacy can and does fuel long-standing feelings of neglect within the North American library community (Apostle and Raymond 1997; Manley 1997).

When information educators, even unintentionally, ignore the negative effects on library practice of their program transformations, when they thereby appear to no longer privilege or even prize the education of librarians, the possibility arises that such educators and many of the practitioners they instruct are living their professional lives in different occupational co-cultures. This possibility can reflect a reality whose negative implications should not be underestimated. Without a shared culture and a common professional speech, practitioners unable to see the applicability of the "faculty information language" in their working environment may seek to devise an acceptable solution to the impasse through recourse to another, more widely understood "language" of American and Canadian cultures —the language of the marketplace. Operating through marketplace rules is a way of looking at the world that is commonly understood, even by its opponents, north and south of the shared national boarder.

When applied to professional education, the marketplace philosophy grants the "buyer" or library community the right to demand certain standards of acceptable education from the "seller" or the ALA-system of approved programs offering accredited master's degrees. In such an exchange, the ability of university-based programs to have their way is limited in the area of educating professional librarians since, if dissatisfied, professional library communities have the alternative of resorting to mandated or, more likely, voluntary state or provincial regulation to certify librarian professional status.

In commercial parlance, using the same business model that is so often is taught in ALA-accredited programs, it would be understandable if American and Canadian library communities decide, as they seem to be doing so at the present time, to hold ALA and its system of accredited education to professionally identified *specifications* for educational adequacy. As will be further explored in this work, such a commonsense approach is currently discouraged by ALA standards that let each program determine what it will teach.

Although far from a supporter of library education and a clear opponent of accreditation, Saracevic (1994, 192) rightly asserts that the 1992 accreditation standards currently in force continue the philosophy evident in the 1972 version. The effects of this philosophy have long been debated, with contemporary commentators seeing the result as a faculty-led effort to minimize appropriate library education (Cox 2006) and others as resistance to imposing a mental straightjacket on faculty (Cronin 2000). The contemporary reality is that allowing every program accredited by the ALA to define its own mission virtually insures that many will not tie the education they provide to identified library needs (Broderick 1997).

The present situation involving librarians, information educators, and information specialists resembles in miniature the conflict between Democrats and Republicans described by *New York Times* columnist David Brooks in "A Polarized America" (2004). Like the members of America's major national political parties, individuals viewing themselves as either librarians or information specialists filter the day-to-day details of reality through their preferred identities. Simply put, in their professional lives librarians and information specialists often see the same things quite differently. The varying mental models involved in such filtering, at bottom, reflect the range of differences separating the fields of library science and information science.

As will be explored throughout the remainder of this work, most explicitly in Chapter 6, it is necessary both to understand the causes of such differences and to develop methods for their accommodation lest they lead to negative consequences for educators and practitioners alike. In American and Canadian cultures the possibility of professional librarianship surviving without an agreed-upon professional education is, at best, problematic. It is also the case that losing their present share of the "market" for professional librarians will do little to promote the longevity of ALA-accredited programs.

REFERENCES

American Library Association. 1992. *Standards for Accreditation of Master's Programs in Library & Information Studies.* Chicago: Office for Accreditation, American Library Association.

Apostle, Richard, and Boris Raymond. 1997. *Librarianship and the Information Paradigm.* Lanham, MD: Scarecrow Press.

Argyris, Chris. 1999. Tacit knowledge and management. In *Tacit Knowledge in Professional Practice: Researcher and Practitioner Perspectives,* edited by Robert J. Sternberg and Joseph A. Horvath, 123–140. Mahwah, NJ: Lawrence Erlbaum Associates.

Augst, Thomas, and Wayne Wiegand. 2001. *The Library as an Agency of Culture.* Lawrence, KS: American Studies. Reprint of the fall 2001 issue of *American Studies* 42, no. 3.

Bates, Marcia J. 1999. The invisible substrate of information science. *Journal of the American Society for Information Science* 50, no. 12 (October): 1043–1050.

Becker, Howard S. 1998. *Tricks of the Trade: How to Think about Your Research While You're Doing It.* Chicago: University of Chicago Press.

Berry, John N. III. 2006. Can ALA bring change? *Library Journal* 131, no. 15 (15 September), http://www.libraryjournal.com/article/CA6370229.html (accessed February 1, 2007).

Broady-Preston, Judith. 2006. CILIP: A twenty-first century association for the information profession? *Library Management* 27 (1/2): 48–65.

Broderick, Dorothy M. 1997. Turning library into a dirty word: A rant. *Library Journal* 122, no. 12 (July), 42–43.

Brooks, David. 2004. A polarized America. Special issue on discourse and democracy. *Hedgehog Review* 6, no. 3: 14–23. Based on the transcript of the Labrosse-Levinson Lecture delivered by David Brooks at the University of Virginia on October 20, 2004.

Budd, John M. 2004. Relevance: Language, semantics, philosophy. *Library Trends* 52, no. 3 (winter): 447–462.

Buschman, John E. 2003. *Dismantling the Public Sphere: Situating and Sustaining Librarianship in the Age of the New Public Philosophy.* Westport, CT: Libraries Unlimited.

Corcoran, Mary, Lynn Dagar, and Anthea Stratigos. 2000. The changing roles of information professionals: Excerpts from an Outsell, Inc. study. *Online* (March/April): 29–30, 32–34.

Cox, Richard J. 2006. Why survival is not enough. *American Libraries* 37, no. 6 (June/July): 42–44.

Cronin, Blaise. 1995. Cutting the Gordian knot. *Information Processing & Management,* 31, no. 6 (November): 897–902.

———. 2000. Quis custodiet custodes? *International Journal of Information Management* 20, no. 4 (August): 311–313.

Crowley, Bill. 1994. Library lobbying as a way of life. *Public Libraries* 33, no. 2 (March–April): 96–98.

———. 1999a. Building useful theory: Tacit knowledge, practitioner reports, and the culture of LIS inquiry. *Journal of Education for Library and Information Science* 40, no. 4 (fall): 282–295.

———. 1999b. The control and direction of professional education. *Journal of the American Society for Information Science* 50, no. 12 (October): 1127–1135.

———. 2000. Tacit knowledge and quality assurance: Bridging the theory-practice divide. In *Knowledge Management for the Information Professional,* ed. T. Kanti Srikantaiah and Michael E. D. Koenig, 205–220. Medford, NJ: Published for the American Society for Information Science by Information Today.

———. 2003. The suicide of the public librarian. *Library Journal* 128 (15 April): 48–49.

———. 2005a. Save professionalism. *Library Journal* (1 September): 46–48.

———. 2005b. *Spanning the Theory-Practice Divide in Library and Information Science.* Lanham, MD: Scarecrow Press.

———. 2006. Suicide prevention. *Library Administration & Management* 20, no. 2 (spring): 75–80.

Cunningham, Anne, and Keith Stanovich. 1998. What reading does for the mind. *American Educator* 22, no. 1–2 (spring–summer): 1–8.

Deane, Gary. 2003. Bridging the value gap: Getting past professional values to customer value in the public library. *Public Libraries* 42, no.5 (September–October): 315–319.

Earned degrees conferred, 2003–4. 2006. *Chronicle of Higher Education* 53, no. 1 (25 August): 22.

Garrison, Dee. 1979. *Apostles of Culture: The Public Librarian and American Society, 1876–1920.* New York: Free Press.

Gorman, Michael. 2000. *Our Enduring Values: Librarianship in the 21st Century.* Chicago: American Library Association.

———. 2004. Whither library education? *New Library World* 105, nos. 1204/1205 (September): 376–380.

Great Britain. Parliament. House of Commons. Culture, Media and Sport Committee. 2005. *Public Libraries,* vol. 2. London: Stationary Office. http://www.publications.parliament.uk/pa/cm200405/cmselect/cmcumeds/81/81i.pdf (accessed January 27, 2007).

Harmon, Glynn, ed. 2006a. Introduction. The first I-conference of the I-school communities. Special section, *Bulletin of the American Society for Information Science and Technology* (April/May): 9–10.

———. ed. 2006b. The first I-Conference of the I-school communities. Special section, *Bulletin of the American Society for Information Science and Technology* (April/May): 9–23.

Hennen, Thomas J. Jr. 2006. Hennen's American Public Library Ratings 2006. *American Libraries* 37, no. 10 (November): 40–42.

Letters. *Library Journal*, July 15, 2003, and July 15, 2003.

Library of Congress, Congressional Research Service. 1986. *Research Policies for the Social and Behavioral Sciences: Report.* Science policy study, no. 6. Washington: U.S. Government Printing Office.

Manley, Will. 1997. Patron revolt. *Booklist* 93 (1 May): 1464.

Matthew, Cynthia T., Anne T Cianciolo, and Robert J Sternberg. 2005. *Developing Effective Military Leaders: Facilitating the Acquisition of Experience Based Tacit Knowledge.* Alexandria, VA: U.S. Army Research Institute for the Behavioral and Social Sciences.

McCabe, Ronald B. 2001. *Civic Librarianship: Renewing the Social Mission of the Public Library.* Lanham, MD: Scarecrow Press.

McGarry, Kevin. 2000. Professional education: Some reflections. *Education for Information* 18, no. 2/3: 105–113.

Mulvaney, John Philip, and Dan O'Connor. 2006. The crux of our crisis. *American Libraries* June/July: 38–40.

Raymond, Boris. 1997. Chapter 1, Paradigms in conflict. In *Librarianship and the Information Paradigm,* ed. Richard Apostle and Boris Raymond, 1–36. Lanham, MD: Scarecrow Press.

Ross, Catherine Sheldrick, Lynne (E.F.) McKechnie, and Paulette M. Rothbauer. 2006. *Reading Matters: What the Research Reveals about Reading, Libraries, and Community.* Westport, CT: Libraries Unlimited.

Rothstein, Samuel. 1985. Why people really hate library schools. *Library Journal* 110, no. 6 (1 April): 41–48.

Rubin, Richard E. 2004. *Foundations of Library and Information Science,* 2nd ed. New York: Neal-Schuman.

Saracevic, Tefko. 1994. Closing of library schools in North America: What role accreditation? *Libri* 44, no. 3 (September): 190–200.

Singer, Benjamin D. 1996. Towards sociology of standards: Problems of a criterial society. *Canadian Journal of Sociology* 21 (2): 203–221.

Whitson, Bill. 1995. Do we have a future? *CARL Newsletter* 18 (3) (September). http://www.carl-acrl.org/Archives/ConferencesArchive/Conference95/future .html (accessed 1/29/07).

Wiegand, Wayne A. 2001. Missing the real story: Where library and information science fails the library profession. In *The Readers' Advisor's Companion,* ed. Kenneth D. Shearer and Robert Burgin, 7–14. Englewood, CO: Libraries Unlimited.

——. 2003. To reposition a research agenda: What American Studies can teach the LIS community about the library I the life of the user. *Library Quarterly* 73, no. 4 (October): 369–382.

——. 2005. Critiquing the curriculum. *American Libraries* 36, no. 1 (January): 58, 60–61.

CHAPTER 3

*"What's the Story?"**

SCENARIO: A CATALOGER'S DISPARAGEMENT OF CHILDREN'S LIBRARIANSHIP

Not that long ago the author had one of those spontaneous conversations that happen with strangers and friends alike at sites as varied as conference convention centers or hotel lobbies. It was a totally unscheduled exchange with an educator holding an appointment with a program offering an American Library Association–accredited master's degree. This professor is proud of her specialty, which involves teaching and researching in such areas as organization of knowledge and metadata management. She unexpectedly sought another professor's understanding for what she viewed as a grievous professional affront that occurred during a talk with her dean over the relative importance of various aspects of the library and information curriculum.

Her outrage barely under control, this professor objected to her dean's assertion that educating librarians to meet the library needs of children and teens is every bit as important as instructing them in the techniques and theories of organizing knowledge within the physical and electronic worlds. It was a claim that this professor saw as intolerable. In consequence, knowing that the author was a library theorist, she both cornered him and demanded that he agree with the righteousness of her protest.

The author thus constituted a captive audience as this outraged academic repeated in detail the arguments she had made to her dean, most of which seem to involve variations on the theme that catalogers were simply more intelligent than all other librarians, particularly children's librarians. Thus constrained, the author took time to reflect on the interests of the administrator whose views were under attack.

---

* "What's the story?", the critical question of business executive Avram Goldberg, lies at the heart of the "Goldberg Rule" for problem solving recommended by Richard E. Neustadt and Ernest R. May in their *Thinking in Time: The Uses of History for Decision Makers* (1986, 105–106).

It is important to note that the dean in question had spent much of her career as a library practitioner. Presuming that she had kept up with the literature after reentering the academic world, it was possible that her defense of the work of children's and teen librarians might have been fueled by recent research on the enormous worth of youth services in promoting literacy, perhaps including the findings so well presented by Stephen D. Krashen in *The Power of Reading: Insights from the Research* (2004) or by Catherine Sheldrick Ross, Lynne (E.F.) McKechnie, and Paulette M. Rothbauer in *Reading Matters: What the Research Reveals about Reading, Libraries, and Community* (2006). The latter work, produced by what might be termed the "Canadian school" of reading researchers, academics with appointments at the University of Western Ontario or the University of Toronto, is emerging as a fundamentally important resource for evaluating the critical roles of libraries and librarians in developing and sustaining literacy over the human lifetime.

As this writer had long ago grown very weary of the tendency of some information educators to minimize the value of library work, he found it impossible to resist reminding the protesting professor of the research recently published by the Online Computer Library Center (OCLC), in *College Students' Perceptions of Libraries and Information Resources: A Report to the OCLC Membership* (2006) and *Perceptions of Libraries and Information Resources: A Report to the OCLC Membership* (2005). Taken together, these works present the results of an extended international study demonstrating, among other findings, that computer-literate adults largely ignore library catalogs and databases and effectively use search engines such as Google to meet their information needs.

This information only enhanced the outrage of the already fuming cataloging instructor, as did this writer's attempt at concluding words, "We have it from OCLC itself. Cataloging is finished. *C'est fini.*"

This flippant response brought about a repeat of the impassioned arguments accompanied by the demand that this writer needed to go online and visit certain academic library Web sites demonstrating how metadata organizers were bringing together information sources from library catalogs, licensed databases, and Internet search engines to meet the needs of inquirers. A response arguing in favor of the importance of early reading encouragement as a cornerstone of librarianship and a foundation for using any electronic tool effectively was impatiently dismissed by this professor. Instead, she stressed the foundational role that organization of knowledge—the modernized version of old-fashioned cataloging—played in developing what this writer sees as the rival field of information science. As might be expected, the exchange ended without any shared basis for agreement.

LATER REFLECTIONS ON THE HALLWAY ENCOUNTER

In retrospect, this professor's arguments for the preeminence of classifying information may seriously overvalue the role of cataloging or organization of knowledge in contributing to the development of information science theory. While researching this present work the writer again read the crucial report of Jonathan R. Cole, the provost who closed down Columbia University's School of Library Service (Cole 1990). In this document, the Ivy League provost claimed that in the minds of outside consultants, the members of a university study committee examining the future of the school, and in his own opinion, connecting "bibliographic control"—another name for enhanced cataloging or what many now term the organization of metadata—to information science was, at best, problematic (1990). In other words, cataloging or organization of knowledge might not be true information science and, in consequence, can be consigned by information theorists to the oft-denigrated world (in information circles) of librarianship.

At a minimum, the exchange with the information science professor over what she saw as her dean's undervaluation of knowledge organization and overestimation of teen and children's services in libraries was a useful reminder of the tendency of humans to form pecking orders with themselves on top. It also serves to jog the author's memory concerning the reality that there is a history behind how things came to be in library and information studies education. Discussing how to renew professional librarianship requires an understanding of how the problems and issues relevant to libraries can now be seen by information-oriented academics employed to teach in ALA-accredited master's degrees as minor concerns, hardly worth examining in the much larger information world. There is a certain amount of irony in the fact that such disdain is being expressed by researchers hired into, and sometimes heading, the very programs whose existence resulted from the long struggle of American and Canadian librarians for an appropriate professional education accredited by ALA.

Noteworthy Events with Implications for North American Library and Information Education and Practice

DATE	EVENT
1852	Publication of *Upon the Objects to Be Attained by the Establishment of a Public Library: Report of the Trustees of the Public Library of the City of Boston 1852* (City Document No. 37). This document represents the first extended justification of the American public library as a tax-supported educational institution.
1876	Foundation of the American Library Association, the first national library association.
	Publication of the first edition of the Dewey Decimal Classification (DDC), developed by Melvil Dewey, and organizing recorded knowledge in ten main classes. In the past, mastery of the DDC and the later Library of Congress Classification system was seen as a benchmark of librarian expertise and a fundamental component of professional library education.
	Publication of the landmark *Public Libraries in the United States of America: Their History, Condition, and Management* by the Department of the Interior's Bureau of Education. This was the first national survey of libraries offering service to the "public" and included public, academic, school, and special libraries of all types.
1887	Establishment of the Columbia College (now Columbia University) School of Library Economy by Melvil Dewey. This program, and the library schools established soon thereafter, emphasized teaching of effective library practice, such as cataloging, administration, and collection development, to what some scholars saw as the detriment of library theory (Biggs 1985). Later, courses dealing with guiding readers, including children and adults, library and book history, and other relevant areas would be added (Reece 1936). Shortly after its founding, Dewey's school was moved to the State Library in Albany and operated as the New York State Library School before merging with the Library School of the New York Public Library and rejoining Columbia in 1926 as the School of Library Service. It was finally closed by Columbia University in 1993 for being nonresponsive to the demands of the university administration that it cease library education, except for the education of academic librarians, and

become a research-intensive *information* school producing information scholars and organizational information specialists (Cole 1990).

1904   Beginning of Canadian library education with a three-week summer school at McGill University (McNally 2004, 208).

1909   The Special Libraries Association (SLA) is officially established. The formation of this organization is the result, in part, of the perception that meeting the information needs of private, corporate, and other organizations differs from providing academic, public, or school library educational, informational, and recreational services to students, educators, and the general public.

1915   Foundation of the Association of American Library Schools. In 1983 it changed its name to the Association for Library and Information Science Education (ALISE).

1923   Publication of Charles C. Williamson's *Training for Library Service: A Report Prepared for the Carnegie Corporation of New York*. Based on the author's research on behalf of the Carnegie Corporation, this report stressed the need to replace library schools controlled by public libraries and the traditional library apprenticeship system with programs affiliated with institutions of higher education.

1924   Creation of Board of Education for Librarianship by ALA as a mechanism for raising the standards of professional education for librarianship. Became the Committee on Accreditation in 1956.

1926   The Graduate Library School (GLS) of the University of Chicago was established with support from a grant from the Carnegie Corporation. By design, "contrary to the expectation of the profession" the initial faculty was not drawn from librarianship but from such fields as "bibliography, history, education, psychology, and sociology. The dual purposes were to promote research and "jar the profession out of its prolonged devotion to the practical techniques set up by Dewey" (Wilson 1949, 52–53). Accredited by ALA from 1932/33, the school was discontinued in 1990 and closed December 1991.

1936   Publication in the April 1 issue of *Library Journal* of Louis R. Wilson's "The Next Fifty Years" in which he discerns an adherence by the younger members of the library profession to formulating a philosophy of the library as an educational institution.

1937   Foundation of the American Documentation Institute (ADI) which played a generative role in the development of the

American variant of information science and, at present, operates as the American Society for Information Science and Technology (ASIS&T).

1945   Appearance of Vannevar Bush's "As We May Think" in the July issue of *Atlantic Monthly*. This article describes the potential for developing a "memex" machine to provide a researcher with desktop access to the world of recorded knowledge. Although its influence is disputed within information circles, the article has long been considered as a milestone in proclaiming to a mass readership the concept of automated access to knowledge without librarians as information intermediaries.

1950   Publication of *The Public Library in the United States: The General Report of the Public Library Inquiry* (Leigh 1950). This summary of the work of the Public Library Inquiry (1947–1950) privileged the public library's information role, classified its educational and learning function as a secondary activity, and dismissed the library's recreational commitment (lending popular books, etc.) as detrimental to its survival in the new communications age (Crowley 2005b).

1953/1955   Coining of the terms "information scientist" (1953) and "information science" (1955). These formulations were developed, in part, to distinguish the activities of information professionals from librarians and their perceived negative image (Summers et al. 1999).

1971   Publication of George J. Stigler's seminal work, "The Theory of Economic Regulation," in the *Bell Journal of Economics and Management Science*. This article is foundational to the study of "regulatory capture" wherein a regulated "industry" more or less controls such regulation and thereby makes sure that the process is "designed and operated primarily for its benefit" (3).

1994   Ending of accreditation for the program at the University of California–Berkeley, following the prior decision of the university chancellor not to apply for the new accreditation deemed necessary by ALA after the university's reorientation of the school to an information focus.

2000   Publication of *Educating Library and Information Science Professionals for a New Century: The KALIPER Report.* (KALIPER 2000). Supported by the W. K. Kellogg Foundation, the process resulting in this report confirmed and encouraged the effort to transform programs of library education into multidisciplinary information schools where library concerns may not be the predominant area of faculty interest.

2004	Adoption of the Library Practitioner Core Competencies (LPCCs) by the Western Council of State Libraries. The competencies, addressing the skills and knowledge required to direct a small public library, are not tied to degrees offered by programs accredited by ALA and may be acquired in other contexts (Helmick and Swigger 2006).
2005–2006	Term of office of noted information critic Michael Gorman as president of ALA.
2005	First I-Conference of the I-School Deans' Community held at Penn State University.
	Publication of *Perceptions of Libraries and Information Resources: A Report to the OCLC Membership* a study of online users in Australia, Canada, India, Singapore, United Kingdom, and United States that revealed the irrelevance of the library as a source of information to many information consumers who preferred doing their own research on the World Wide Web.
2006	Publication of *Reading Matters: What the Research Reveals About Reading, Libraries and Community.*
	Publication of *Reading Between the Lines: What the ACT Reveals About College Readiness in Reading,* a study exposing the reality "only 51 percent of ACT-tested high school graduates are ready for college-level reading" (ACT 2006, 7).

PUBLIC EXPECTATIONS, INFORMATION EDUCATION, AND LIBRARY PRACTICE: THE START OF ALA ACCREDITATION

The 1924 "Report of the Temporary Library Training Board" to the ALA Council served as the catalyst for the Association to create the permanent Board of Education for Librarianship, a body which evolved into the present ALA Committee on Accreditation. In this report the planning body identified "two fundamental convictions regarding libraries and library service." These included

1. The increasing appreciation of libraries as an important component of the nation's educational system;
2. The centrality to "good libraries and good library service" of first-rate and thoroughly educated librarians (Temporary Library Training Board 1924, 257).

This emphasis on libraries as fundamental to the American educational system in the report that generated the system of ALA accreditation would not have been unexpected to its readers. Philosophically, it restated the emphasis on the roles of libraries and librarians in support of learning that had gained traction in late nineteenth- and early twentieth-century academic, public, and school environments. This emphasis on the educational roles of librarians and libraries had been the basis on which progressive government officials, community opinion leaders, and members of the general public justified tax support of the nation's growing public library system, and was similarly used by public school and academic administrators to foster the development of school and academic libraries.

As far back as 1852 the trustees of the Boston Public Library argued that the same reasons for public support of elementary education applied to funding a public library in their catalytic *Upon the Objects to be Attained by the Establishment of a Public Library: Report of the Trustees of the Public Library of the City of Boston, July 1852*. Nearly a quarter century later, the editors of the monumental 1876 *Public Libraries in the United States of America*—both nonlibrarians—emphasized the "influence of the librarian as educator" and observed "for forty years the importance of public libraries as auxiliaries to public education has been recognized and dwelt upon by American educators whenever common schools have flourished" (Warren and Clark 1876, xi).

The connection of libraries, particularly academic, school, and public libraries, with education still represents the conventional wisdom of the American public and indeed much of the developed world. As a public policy preference, it was restated as recently as February 3, 2006, by Governor Kathleen Sebelius of Kansas who observed, "Libraries provide Kansans of all ages with the opportunity to learn and to explore. The help us broaden our knowledge and provide a window to the world. . . . A good library enriches lives by promoting life-long learning" (Kansas 2006).

One of the more interesting and persuasive studies confirming the perception of libraries as places for learning was recently conducted on a global basis and reported in a rather large document titled *Perceptions of Libraries and Information Resources: A Report to the OCLC Membership*, published in 2005 by OCLC. It was based on data collected by Harris Poll Online and involving 3,348 English-speakers, male and female, eighteen years and older, with Internet access and living in Australia, Canada, India, Singapore, the United Kingdom, and the United States (xi).

The results of this survey were analyzed in depth by OCLC staff possessing a strong business perspective and a number of MBA degrees (title page). They concluded that the data demonstrated the following.

- *The "library" is a single brand.* People see all of all types of libraries as, in effect, a single organization, "one entity with many outlets—constant, consistent, expected. The 'Library' is, in essence, a global brand: a brand dominated by nostalgia and reinforced by common experience" (6-8).
- *Libraries are not really used as a source of electronic information.* While as many as 50 percent of the respondents saw that "information" was the main purpose of the library—as opposed to a third who still indicated "books"—this information-oriented response broke down when it was revealed that "the majority of information seekers are not making much use of the array of electronic resources (online magazines, databases, and reference assistance, for example) libraries make available" (6-4).
- *Google and other search engines own the electronic information world or what OCLC terms the "infosphere."* "There is widespread use of [non-Library] Internet information resources. Respondents regularly use search engines, email and instant messages to obtain and share information" (6-4).

So, what do people expect from this thing we call "the library"? As noted by OCLC

> When prompted, information consumers see libraries' role in the *community as a place to learn, as a place to read, as a place to make information freely available, as a place to support literacy, as a place to provide research support, as a place to provide free computer Internet access* and more. These library services are relevant and differentiated. (6-8; emphasis in original)

A place to learn? A place to read? A place to support literacy? Such perceptions do not appear to be coming from respondents who see the "library" as "global brand" to meet their needs as "information consumers." Rather they seem to be responses from people who see the "library" as vital to their roles as lifelong learners and readers, categories that, at times, research reveals to be nearly identical (Ross, McKechnie, and Rothbauer 2006). From the perspective of those who tie the library to the role of information provider, the results of the OCLC study comes fairly close to an unmitigated disaster. Conversely, from the point of view of those who envision the library as a preeminent lifelong learning facilitator the study has the happy result of reporting that people see the mass of library services as part of a self-education or learning process that particularly prizes the library's role in advancing reading.

On occasion challenges to the beliefs on which academics have developed their careers will be taken seriously by those so confronted (Kuhn 1970). The more thoughtful members of the information science community who have identified "library" with "information" might yet feel compelled to address the reality that attempts to "brand" the library as a twenty-first-century information provider seem to be irrelevant to computer-literate English speakers in developed nations, specifically including Canada and the United States. As described by the OCLC staff analysts in the "Conclusions and Observations" section of *Perceptions of Libraries and Information Resources*, rejuvenation of the "library" brand will require discarding the comforting yet erroneous view of the library as Internet reference provider of choice and

- Accepting the fruitlessness of trying to refocus the "habits and lifestyles" of Internet users away from search engines and toward the library's electronic resources. Changing consumer lifestyles is enormously difficult even with the greater resources available to the private sector, a reality so common that it is matter-of-factly discussed in daily newspapers (Chandler 2006);
- Redesigning print and digital library services to "reconstruct" the experience of using the library;
- Emphasizing the role of libraries as "gathering places within the community or university";
- Building on consumer perceptions of the library as a place, as noted above, to
  - Learn,
  - Read,
  - Make information freely available,
  - Support literacy,
  - Provide research support,
  - Provide free computer access,
  - And more (6-8).

A NATIONAL CRISIS WITH READING

Shortly after the results of the massive OCLC study were presented to the world, the U.S. Department of Education issued *A Test of*

Leadership: Charting the Future of U. S. Higher Education: A Report of the Commission Appointed by Secretary of Education Margaret Spellings (2006). Among the findings documented by the commission are both problems and possibilities amenable to being addressed by a library "brand" based on learning and reading. These included the realities that

- "just 36 percent [of high school seniors] are proficient in reading" according to the National Assessment of Educational Progress (NAEP) (6);
- "reading books that weren't assigned in class" helps determine "the value and quality of . . . [the student] undergraduate experience" according to the National Survey of Student Engagement (NSSE) and Community College Survey of Student Engagement (CCSSE) (23);
- "many students who do earn degrees have not actually mastered the reading, writing, and thinking skills we expect of college graduates. Over the past decade, literacy among college graduates has actually declined" (x).

When the results of OCLC's and Department of Education's studies are read in conjunction with the recent findings of ACT, published in *Reading Between the Lines: What the ACT Reveals about College Readiness in Reading,* that "only 51 percent of 2005 ACT-tested high school graduates are ready for college-level reading" (2006, 1) it becomes abundantly clear that the United States is suffering from a combination learning and reading crisis of truly significant proportions.

One would think that such a massive, society-wide reading problem would give rise to solutions developed across the spectrum of the library community. After all, weren't academic, public, and school libraries, as well as the system of ALA accreditation of library education itself, called into being with a learning, specifically reading mandate (*Upon the Objects to be Attained by the Establishment of a Public Library* 1852; Temporary Library Training Board 1924)? Haven't the programs offering ALA-accredited master's degrees been turning out academic and public librarians superbly equipped to work with their school library colleagues to address the literacy and learning issues so well identified, almost to the level of redundancy, by OCLC, the Department of Education, and ACT? Will it not be the case that responding to these reading and other educational challenges, so vital to both individual success and national well-being, will serve to keep the library "brand" relevant and library professionalism valued throughout the twenty-first century?

Unfortunately, any optimistic assertions regarding the ability of librarians educated in programs accredited to offer ALA-approved master's degrees to address the fundamentally important issues of reading and learning would be grievously in error. The reason for this regrettable state of affairs is simple to relate. In a period where concerns regarding upgrading the reading and learning effectiveness of students and the general public now bedevil university presidents, state governors, provincial politicians, and parents alike, many ALA-accredited programs have changed their emphasis away from such cultural priorities. Instead of educating "librarians" qualified to encourage reading and learning, the courses leading to ALA-accredited degrees have been molding "information specialists" through the study of theories regarding how information is generated, accumulated, organized, stored, disseminated, and, ultimately, either archived or removed from a given information system.

Transforming Library to Information Education

Consideration of how education for librarianship was transformed into what ALA euphemistically terms "library and information studies" might best begin with reviewing the official description of the field. Although the published *Standards for Accreditation of Master's Programs in Library & Information Studies 1992* is in the process of being revised as of this writing (2007), the subcommittee charged with leading the effort sees the updating as "fairly minor" (Standards Review Subcommittee 2006). More to the point, the actual definition of library and information studies remains unchanged.

According to the ALA (1992),

> The phrase "library and information studies" is understood to be concerned with recordable information and knowledge and the services and technologies to facilitate their management and use. Library and information studies encompasses information and knowledge creation, communication, identification, selection, acquisition, organization, storage and retrieval, preservation, analysis, interpretation, evaluation, synthesis, dissemination, and management. (2)

Readers might wonder how this ALA-approved definition of "library and information studies," a description undoubtedly developed to stake a claim for intellectual "territory" within the modern university, differs from any of the numerous definitions of "information science." In point of fact, if the two instances of "library" were removed from the description of the field, it probably would be an "information" definition more or less acceptable to many information scholars. And therein lies the problem. It is a concept of the field that provides virtually no intellectual support for addressing the bulk of the relevant library research questions and, equally if not more important, it offers little or no assistance for addressing many of the problems that academic, public, and school librarians are being asked to help solve by elements of the larger American and Canadian cultures.

The absence of library theory for guiding practitioners in addressing cultural problems dealing with reading and lifelong learning means, for example, that first-rate works such as Ross, McKechnie, and Rothbauer's *Reading Matters: What the Research Reveals about Reading, Libraries, and Community* (2006) are notable for their rarity. It is similarly reflected in the fact that Michael K. Buckland's "Five Grand Challenges for Library Research" is forced to discuss decades-old research on reading, a demonstration of how far library and information studies has wandered from its initial commitment to validating the roles of librarians in promoting reading within their varied communities (2003, 678). Understandings that library and information scholars have defaulted from the challenge of assisting practitioners to improve and justify their efforts to help solve societal problems with reading and lifelong learning are not new. In his fundamentally important 1982 study *Reading Research and Librarianship: A History and Analysis,* Stephen Karetzky made the crucial point that the early research by library educators into reading has not been effectively followed up. "Great advances" have been lacking since the 1930s, and "research on the psychology of reading, reading motivation, and the individual and social effects of reading is still needed" (357).

In Chapter 6 the author will address the synergies possible between library encouragement of computer gaming and reading as representing but one approach to research that could help American and Canadian cultures solve critical problems with reading and lifelong learning. Such advances, it must be stressed, will require less of an emphasis on information provision and more of an updating of classical library reading models.

An Overabundance of "Information" Education?

Although information advocates tend to portray the effort to secure or restore appropriate professional education at the university
level as a struggle between the "academic and professional communities" (Cronin 2000, 2002) it can come as a shock to some that the national culture of the United States recognizes more than two parties
with a valid interest in appropriately educated professional librarians.
In the U.S. context, these include (1) professionals working in academic environments, in either a research/teaching faculty or academic
librarian capacity; (2) librarian or information professionals employed
off-campus in a range of positions, including administrative; (3) state
residents and their elected officials; and (4) the citizenry and nation as
a whole (Crowley 2005a). Although often ignored by faculty in research universities, except when their demands for more public resources or academic freedom are not deemed to be a priority, the influence of citizens and their elected officials in the debate over relevant
professional education in the North American context should not be
underestimated.

As recently as the mid-1990s the State of Ohio's Board of Regents
and state universities were forced to respond to legislative outrage
over the use of withheld state dollars that had been restored in subsequent university budgets after a national economic recession. Instead
of being applied to increasing undergraduate enrollments these rein-
stated funds were used to support Ph.D. students, many of whom were
not from Ohio. Although a clear priority of universities interested in
research, this was considered an affront to both state residents and
elected officials whose shared priority was the use of these same dollars for increasing the enrollment of undergraduate students, most of
whom were the daughters and sons of Ohio taxpayers. In the course of
the dispute, the Board of Regents was forced to undertake evaluations
of certain Ph.D. programs in state-assisted universities. A number of
these doctoral programs were deemed to be excessive for Ohio's needs
and lost their state subsidies. Additionally, since it was perceived that
certain academic units had allowed faculty members to reduce the number of classes taught, presumably in order to conduct more research, a
law was passed increasing faculty teaching loads by 10 percent.

Although the Ohio Board of Regents carried out excellent damage
control, the revelation of the gulf between faculty self-interest (Ph.D.

programs that attract out-of-state students who help with faculty research) and citizen priorities (educating more Ohio undergraduate students) was one of those "exposures [that] are dangerous for higher education, since they carry with them the risk that the public may see a university or university system as unresponsive to its demands, a perception that rarely has positive implications for funding" (Crowley 2005a, 135–136).

Of late, what Mark D. Bowles (1999) described as the "information wars," or the dispute between librarians/humanists and documentalists/scientists over "information retrieval" (156), has exploded into a competition for educating students and conducting research in information or informatics across campuses. Motivated by the computer/Internet/Web revolutions and the financial lure of a globalized information economy, fields and disciplines throughout higher education now claim both the right and ability to teach information competence. It has become a challenge that extends far beyond the bounds of "library and information studies" or "information science." One wonders, for instance, if the failed effort by former Chancellor Sharon Brehm of Indiana University (IU), Bloomington, to encourage merging the university's Department of Computer Science and the School of Library and Information Science (SLIS) into the School of Informatics (Crowley 2004), represents an effort to deal with perhaps unnecessary duplication in information-informatics education and thereby reduce costs to the institution. Since some SLIS faculty members at Indiana University hold dual appointments with either the Department of Computer Science or the School of Informatics, such an approach might make a great deal of sense except for the matter of providing appropriate education for academic, public, and school librarians, whose concerns far exceed the constraints of the information paradigm.

The early twenty-first century is a time when use of a search engine to find out where one might be educated for careers in information, as well as biological, dental, legal, medical, nursing, and other types of "informatics"—briefly defined as the application of computers to the study of information in general or in a given field—reveals numerous courses, degrees, and other sources of instruction. Frequently, these degrees and certificates are offered by fields and disciplines whose departments, schools, or colleges lack ALA accreditation (United States and Canada) or any history of library education (elsewhere in the world). Within the Canadian environment, for example, a search of the Association of Universities and Colleges of Canada's database *Directory of Canadian Universities* in the fields of "Information Resources Management/CIO Training" and "Information Science/Studies" can even bring up a majority of degrees from schools lacking ALA endorsement (Association of Universities and Colleges of Canada 2006). Within such a competitive environment for teaching and researching information, the professional education of librarians may represent one of the few ways of distinguishing "information" programs accredited by ALA from their broad range of information and informatics competitors.

Such duplication among "information" programs is nothing new. Writing in the April/May 1992 issue of the *Bulletin of the American Society for Information Science,* Thomas J. Galvin noted that the

- American Assembly of Collegiate Schools of Business accredited programs offering the MIS or management information systems degree;
- Computing Science Accreditation Board oversaw computer science programs and such programs "in many cases overlap with information science";
- National Association of Schools of Public Affairs and Administration supervised "information resource management" in master of public administration programs;
- Accreditation Board for Engineering and Technology accredited "electrical, computer and telecommunications engineering education" (20).

Even a decade and a half ago, Galvin warned that the information education competition could seize control over "professional education in our own field" (20).

In addition to cautioning against the information education competition Galvin, presumably because he was writing in an information science publication, the *Bulletin of the American Society for Information Science,* was sufficiently comfortable to explain the tactical reasons why even an information supporter such as himself could live with the term "library and information studies" instead of "information studies" in the 1992 ALA Standards for Accreditation. These reasons, it should be noted, are fully in accord with an old political maxim, explained to the author by a congressional aide over coffee during a long-ago ALA National Library Legislative Day in Washington, DC.

"You can get away with murder so long as you don't call it that," he pointed out in what some might see as the best—and others as the worst—in political calculation.

According to Galvin, information adherents could find the term "library and information studies" acceptable since

1. Accreditation was still the recognized duty of ALA and not assigned to the "American Information Studies Association";
2. Most of the schools with accredited degrees still kept "library" in their names in order "not to appear to have abandoned their traditional constituency";
3. "Library and information studies" was a term that was "politically acceptable to the several constituencies," presumably including self-styled librarians, which would have to approve the Standards for Accreditation;
4. The ALA operated the "only accreditation game in town" (20).

Since Galvin's article several of the leading I-schools (information schools), a number with master's degrees accredited by ALA, have joined in discussions to set up an approach to accrediting degrees in information technology (Burnett and Bonnici 2006). As will be explored in the next chapter, such a development only underscores the necessity for the library community to end the regulatory capture of ALA accreditation and reassume control over library education.

Loss of a Shared Co-Culture

Introducing the Problem

With Galvin's reminder of the preference of many information theorists to define "library" as "information"—no matter how irrelevant the forced amalgamation might be—it is useful to draw on the fields of communications and anthropology to bring the concepts of culture and co-cultures into the discussion. The simplest definition of culture the author has encountered was offered by Ralph Nicholas—"the whole way of life of a particular human society" (1991, 16). This definition includes everything from what one wears and eats, to the language one speaks, one's attitude toward religion and an afterlife, who one marries, where one is born, and how one is buried. It includes forms of courtesy, preferred occupations, whether or not one salutes a flag or burns it, and even whether one defines one's field as "librarianship" or "information."

The first point to be made is that cultures are not monolithic. Although one culture is usually portrayed as a national culture, there are countless competing and subordinate entities known as co-cultures. According to Samovar, Porter, and McDaniel, a co-culture is a term used *"when discussing groups or social communities exhibiting communication characteristics, perceptions, values, beliefs, and practices that are sufficiently different to distinguish them from the other groups, communities, and the dominant culture"* (2007, 11; emphasis in original). The diverse natures of the American and Canadian nations mean their citizens, at one and the same time, can be members of multiple co-cultures that operate under their own rules. In the past it was perfectly possible for a librarian experienced in a number of contexts to earn a Ph.D., become a faculty member in a university offering an ALA-accredited master's degree, and function successfully

- according to university co-culture rules during the day;
- using consultant co-culture standards while advising an academic library planning committee once a week;
- according to the rules of a trustee co-culture after being elected or appointed to a library or school board; and
- working with a public library community's co-cultural orientation while presenting at a state conference.

The key to operating successfully within multiple co-cultures in the larger American or Canadian national cultures is spending enough time in them learning their different "communication characteristics, perceptions, values, beliefs, and practices" (Samovar, Porter, and McDaniel 2007, 11). The concept of co-cultures is absolutely essential to any effort at renewing professional librarianship since, among other understandings, it helps explain what already has been lost. Without a doubt, the primary and growing loss within contemporary ALA-accredited programs is the historic sharing of co-cultures by educators, practitioners, and, in some cases, relevant others. The measure of this loss is the fact that in the past, the definition of library and information studies, however biased towards information, literally did not matter to the library community. This was because the strength of the co-cultures shared by practitioners and researchers was such that faculty teaching and researching in programs offering the ALA-accredited master's degree would find ways of making their instruction relevant to practitioner realities despite having to use fashionable, if irrelevant, information models.

National cultures and its various co-cultures, including the co-cultures supporting libraries and information centers, all have histories. So, too, do the cultures and subcultures of academic fields and disciplines, some of which extend across geographic and institutional boundaries. The present author is far from alone is this discernment. In this context, one vision of the sometimes confounding results of this reality, presented by Michael A. Harris and Stan A. Hannah in their 1993 work *Into the Future: The Foundations of Library and Information Services in the Post-Industrial Era,* is particularly worth noting.

In their work, Harris and Hannah first developed a thoughtful analysis of the contemporary visions of the post-industrial world. Afterward, they combined this consideration with an effective mining of the extensive literature tracing the philosophical justifications for the American library and librarian (and their later information counterparts) from the claims flowing from a nineteenth-century educational allegiance through the implications of the mainstream twentieth-century assertion that libraries, librarians, and information specialists function as unbiased collectors and disseminators of information, and, ultimately, to an examination of the consequences of the contemporary search for professional and institutional relevance in the "information era."

In 1993, Harris and Hannah concluded their work with a call for a "consensus" on the contested concepts of freedom, equality, and neutrality as a "preliminary to establishing a widespread agreement on the mission of the profession in the post-industrial world" (1993, 145). As will be seen, more than a dozen years since the publication of their analysis, the Harris and Hannah call for dialog and debate has a new urgency. It has seemingly acquired a time limit through the intensification of competition with Google and other information providers and has been immensely complicated by the explicit and implicit claims of information adherents within ALA-accredited programs and in the larger world that "information" and not "library" discourse provides the only acceptable channel for discussing library and information futures.

The following chapters will examine the American variant of the international information culture and will also explore the implications for library practice and relevant library education flowing from the loss of co-cultures previously shared among faculty, practitioners, and elected officials, as well as other academic, public, and school library stakeholders. An alternative definition of librarianship reflecting the questions that society has asked librarianship to address and the library education relevant to this effort will also be explored.

References

ACT, Inc. 2006. *Reading Between the Lines: What the ACT Reveals About College Readiness in Reading.* Iowa City, IA: ACT.

American Library Association. 1992. *Standards for Accreditation of Master's Programs in Library & Information Studies.* Chicago: Office for Accreditation, American Library Association.

Association of Universities and Colleges of Canada. *Directory of Canadian Universities.* http://oraweb.aucc.ca/showdcu.html (accessed December 28, 2006).

Biggs, Mary. 1985. Who/what/why should a library educator be? *Journal of Education for Library and Information Science* 25, no. 4 (spring): 262–278.

Bowles, Mark D. 1999. The information wars: Two cultures and the conflict in information retrieval, 1945–1999. in *Proceedings of the 1998 Conference on the History and Heritage of Science Information Systems,* ed. Mary Ellen Bowen, Trudi Bellardo Hahn, Robert V. Williams, 156–166. Medford, NJ: Published for the American Society for Information Science and the Chemical Heritage Foundation by Information Today.

Buckland, Michael K. 2003. Five grand challenges for library research. *Library Trends* 51, no. 4 (spring): 675–686.

Burnett, Kathleen M., and Laurie J. Bonnici. 2006. Contested terrain: Accreditation and the future of the profession of librarianship. *Library Quarterly* 76, no. 2 (April): 193–219.

Bush, Vannevar. 1945. As we may think. *Atlantic Monthly,* July. Atlantic Online http://www.theatlantic.com/doc/print/194507/bush (accessed December 11, 2006).

Chandler, Susan. 2006. To thine own brand be true. *Chicago Tribune,* December 24, 2006, sec. 2, Perspective.

Cole, Jonathan R. 1990. *Report of the Provost on the School of Library Service at Columbia.* New York: Columbia University in the City of New York.

College Students' Perceptions of Libraries and Information Resources: A Report to the OCLC Membership. 2006. Principal contributors, Cathy De Rosa et al. Dublin, OH: OCLC Online Computer Library Center. http://www.oclc.org/reports/perceptionscollege.htm (accessed September 22, 2006).

Cronin, Blaise. 2000. Letter from America: Quis Custodiet custodes? *International Journal of Information Management* 20, no. 4 (August): 311–313.

———. 2002. Holding the center while prospecting at the periphery: Domain identity and coherence in North American information studies education. *Education for Information* 20, no. 1 (March): 3–10.

Crowley, Bill. 2004. Just another field? *Library Journal* 129 (1 November): 44–46.

——. 2005a. *Spanning the Theory-Practice Divide in Library and Information Science.* Lanham, MD: Scarecrow Press.

——. 2005b. Rediscovering the history of readers advisory service. *Public Libraries* 44, no. 1 (January/February): 37–41.

Galvin, Thomas J. 1992. The new ALA standards for accreditation: A personal perspective. *Bulletin of the American Society for Information Science* 18, no. 4 (April/May): 19–20.

Harris, Michael H., and Stan A. Hannah. 1993. *Into the Future: The Foundations of Library and Information Services in the Post-Industrial Era.* Norwood, NJ: Ablex.

Helmick, Catherine, and Keith Swigger. 2006. Core competencies of library practitioners. *Public Libraries* 45, no. 2 (March/April): 54–69.

KALIPER. *Educating Library and Information Science Professionals for a New Century, the KALIPER Report.* 2000. Reston, VA: KALIPER Advisory Committee, Association for Library and Information Science Education (ALISE).

Kansas, Office of the Governor. 2006. Governor's appointees promote libraries as life-long learning resources: Sebelius appoints two, reappoints six to Southeast Regional Library System. News release, February 3, 2006. http://www.governor.ks.gov/news/NewsRelease/2006/nr-06-0203a.html (accessed December 13, 2006).

Karetzky, Stephen. 1982. *Reading Research and Librarianship: A History and Analysis.* Contributions in librarianship and information science, no. 36. Westport, CT: Greenwood Press.

Krashen, Stephen D. 2004. *The Power of Reading: Insights from the Research,* 2nd ed. Westport, CT: Libraries Unlimited.

Kuhn, Thomas S. 1970. *The Structure of Scientific Revolutions,* 2nd ed. Chicago: University of Chicago Press.

Leigh, Robert D. 1950. *The Public Library in the United States: The General Report of the Public Library Inquiry.* New York: Columbia University Press.

McNally, Peter F. 2004. One hundred years of Canadian graduate education for library and information studies. *Feliciter* 50, no. 5: 208–211.

Neustadt, Richard E., and Ernest R. May. 1986. *Thinking in Time: The Uses of History for Decision Makers.* New York: Free Press.

Nicholas, Ralph W. 1991. Cultures in the curriculum. *Liberal Education* 77, no. 3 (May/June): 16–21.

Perceptions of Libraries and Information Resources: A Report to the OCLC Membership. 2005. Principal contributors, Cathy De Rosa et al. Dublin, OH: OCLC Online Computer Library Center. http://www.oclc.org/reports/2005perceptions.htm (accessed September 22, 2006).

Public Libraries in the United States of America: Their History, Condition, and Management. 1876. Ed. S. R. Warren and S. N. Clark. Special report, Department of the Interior, Bureau of Education. Parts I–II. Washington, DC: GPO.

Reece, Ernest J. 1936. *The Curriculum in Library Schools.* New York: Columbia University Press.

Ross, Catherine Sheldrick, Lynne (E.F.) McKechnie, and Paulette M. Rothbauer. 2006. *Reading Matters: What the Research Reveals about Reading, Libraries, and Community*. Westport, CT: Libraries Unlimited.

Samovar, Larry A., Richard E. Porter, Edwin R. McDaniel. 2007. *Communication Between Cultures*, 6th ed. Belmont, CA: Thomson Wadsworth.

Standards Review Committee, American Library Association Committee on Accreditation. 2006. Updating the 1992 *Standards for Accreditation of Master's Programs in Library and Information Studies:* Overview and Comments. http://www.ala.org/ala/accreditation/prp/prismreports.htm (accessed December 19, 2006). Release approved by COA November 18, 2006.

Stigler, George J. 1971. The theory of economic regulation. *Bell Journal of Economics and Management Science* 2, no. 1 (spring): 3–21.

Summers, Ron, Charles Oppenheim, Jack Meadows, Cliff McKnight, and Margaret Kinnell. 1999. Information science in 2010. A Loughborough University view. *Journal of the American Society for Information Science* 50, no. 12 (October): 1153–1162.

Temporary Library Training Board, American Library Association. 1924. Report of the Temporary Library Training Board. *American Library Association Bulletin* 18: 257–288.

United States Department of Education, Secretary of Education's Commission on the Future of Higher Education. 2006. *A Test of Leadership: Charting the Future of U. S. Higher Education: A Report of the Commission Appointed by Secretary of Education Margaret Spellings*. Washington, DC: U.S. Department of Education. http://www. ed.gov/about/bdscomm/list/hiedfuture/reports.html (accessed December 22, 2006).

Upon the Objects to be Attained by the Establishment of a Public Library: Report of the Trustees of the Public Library of the City of Boston, July 1852. Boston Public Library. City Document—No. 27 J.H. Eastburn, City Printer. http://www.scls.lib.wi.us/mcm/history/report_of_trustees.html (accessed December 11, 2006).

Warren, S. R., and S. N. Clark. 1876. Introduction. In *Public Libraries in the United States of America: Their History, Condition, and Management*, ed. S. R. Warren and S. N. Clark. Special report, Department of the Interior, Bureau of Education. Parts I–II. Washington, DC: GPO.

Williamson, Charles Clarence 1971. *The Williamson Reports of 1921 and 1923, Including "Training for Library Work" (1921) and "Training for Library Service" (1923)*. Metuchen, NJ: Scarecrow Press.

Wilson, Louis R. 1936. The next fifty years. *Library Journal* 61, no. 7 (1 April): 255–260.

———. 1949/1971. Historical development of education for librarianship in the United States. In *Education for Librarianship: Papers Presented at the Library Conference, University of Chicago, August 16–21, 1948*, ed. Bernard Berelson, 44–59. Rpt. Freeport, NY: Books for Libraries Press.

CHAPTER 4

The Information–Library Conundrum

GORMAN AND TWO LIBRARY "EDUCATION" STORIES

As of this writing, the influence of former American Library Association president Michael Gorman looms large in any review of the effectiveness and relevance of information education for library practice. Gorman made the reform of ALA-accredited education the central aim of his 2005–2006 presidential year. Prior to his term, at the July 31–August 1, 2003, joint meeting of EUCLID/ALISE (European Association for Library and Information Education and Research and Association for Library and Information Science Education) titled "Coping with Continual Change—Change Management," Gorman raised a number of critical questions, possible answers to which will be suggested throughout the remainder of this work. In his remarks, later printed in the journal *New Library World,* Gorman asked

- Can library education and information science coexist in harmony without detriment to either or must they divorce?
- Can ALA and the LIS schools work together to produce a national core curriculum?
- Can we revamp the accreditation system so that it is based on nationally agreed standards?
- Can we reconceptualize librarianship to make it attractive to future generations of librarians (Gorman 2004, 380)?

Evidence of the gap that needs to be crossed to provide answers satisfactory to both sides can be found in an incident involving a public library director from a state adjacent to Illinois. The dean of the program criticized by the director in the following anecdote was not present to defend the relevance of his program to the realities of the library world. In consequence, the author will not identify either the program or the Midwestern state involved.

Growing Her Own Librarians

Several years ago William Brace, a Dominican University emeritus professor, and the author attended a graduation party for a student with a long career in libraries who had decided in midlife to return to school and earn an ALA-accredited master's degree. The student had started but left her studies at another program decades before, a fact that may have explained the presence of a longtime friend who was a director of a public library in an adjacent state. Halfway through the meal, this visiting library director informed those present that she was giving up hiring graduates from the library and information science program of her state's flagship university and was going to "grow her own librarians." This decision, she related, was in response to the fact that her state's ALA-accredited program, which still had "library" in its name, had taken to relying on computer science and informatics faculty who had little interest in things "library" and, in consequence, did not provide students with an appropriate library education.

Both Brace and the author needed little encouragement to argue this claim with the library director and spent a considerable amount of time discussing the negatives of her plan. It was stressed that if she and her counterparts abandoned the requirement of the ALA-accredited master's degree for librarians, it would result in decreased professionalism, return the preparation of librarians to the apprenticeship system, and result in too strong a reliance on a state certification process that already allows an alternative scheme for preparing directors of smaller public libraries. The inevitable result, it was stressed, would be a reduction in professionalism accompanied by a similar decline in the salaries of the librarians and other library staff.

Such arguments did not seem to have much of an impact on this out-of-state library director's resolution to train her own professional librarians. Eventually, Brace and this author were forced to argue that the library director could write off the professional education provided at her state university and hire graduates from those ALA-accredited programs that still valued a library connection. In response to such arguments, she related that her close-knit community would prefer that she employ local residents who had not attended an ALA-accredited program to importing professionals from other states. As the conversation was ending the director asserted, given what many saw as the flight from a library education of her own state's ALA-accredited program and the very public denigration of librarianship by its dean, that it was an exercise in hypocrisy to keep the word "library" in the name of the school. This view, she insisted, was widely shared among the professional librarians of her state and she would not be the only director resorting to intensive in-service training and the mentoring of new staff in lieu of requiring an irrelevant ALA-accredited master's degree.

A day after this graduation dinner this author looked up the Web page of the state university ALA-accredited program complained about by the library director. Both at that time and currently the school and its dean proclaimed the aim of educating librarians, along with other members of the so-called information professions. Since it is unlikely that prospective students would have heard or read the dean's occasional attacks on librarianship, chances are that such pronouncements, even at their most vituperative, have not affected student enrollment in his program. Would-be librarians can be most practical and enduring the disdain of librarianship expressed by one's dean might be an acceptable trade-off for earning an ALA-accredited degree while paying reduced in-state tuition. Nonetheless, to the extent that the bill of indictment regarding program irrelevance offered by the disillusioned library director was and is true, this incident represents

- yet another example of the professional cognitive dissonance, discussed in Chapter 1 as a result of theories taught by information educators conflicting with academic, public, and school library professional realities;
- a further demonstration, as already considered in Chapter 2, of the operation of Chris Argyris's espoused theory–theory in use divide within organizations offering degrees accredited by ALA. In this instance it may well be the case, regardless of the assertion of the state university that it provides an appropriate library education (espoused theory), that its claim is contradicted by the actual content of the courses offered (theory in use) (Argyris 1999, 126). In other words, the presence of the word "library" in the name of the program and one of its degrees may constitute a higher education version of the proverbial "red herring" diverting attention away from the reality of its abandonment of appropriate education for librarianship.

If the visiting library director was correct in her assertions that an information-centric education within an ALA-accredited program poorly prepares graduates for the realities of library practice, the responsibility for this state of affairs must lie with those who have inappropriately embedded library education in the information model.

A Faculty Discussion on the Jesse Forum

In North America and elsewhere JESSE—the Open Lib/Info Sci Education Forum (jesse@listserv.utk.edu)—is often considered to be a critical resource for the exchange of ideas on both library and information education. As this chapter was being written, a thread appeared on JESSE addressing the concerns of those involved regarding the future of professional *library and information* education. Such concerns, held by a number of library and information educators both within and without programs accredited by ALA, are usually expressed in less public venues. Lee Shiflett, chair of the Department of Library and Information Studies, University of North Carolina at Greensboro, contributed several postings to the Internet thread. His initial submission, dated March 2, 2007, consisted of a thoughtful response to a request for information from another LIS educator. This professor was seeking input on how a LIS program might fare after being made part of college or school of education. Her request followed the previous month's confirmation that the University at Buffalo's School of Informatics would be dissolved and its constituent Department of Communication and Department of Library and Information Studies (DLIS) would be provided with new homes elsewhere in the university (Lorna Peterson to JESSE mailing list, February 22, 2007). The DLIS program, it was reported, is to be incorporated within the Graduate School of Education. In his posting Shiflett went beyond an immediate response to the Buffalo reorganization to raise questions regarding educating librarians at the university level.

Briefly summarized, Shiflett's "mainstream" points about library and information studies education addressed the reality that maintaining independence within the university is not always possible. He further noted that it is difficult to find appropriate academic locations for LIS programs because of their small size, lack of campus influence, and the difficulty of finding appropriately matched partners (Lee Shiflett to JESSE mailing list, March 2, 2007).

It is the author's view that there exists something close to a consensus regarding the preceding within the contemporary communities of library and information educators. However, Shiflett's next points, while much more controversial, might even be endorsed by the public library director who had argued the irrelevance of the information education provided aspiring public librarians by her state's ALA-accredited program (above).

As contended by Shiflett,

- thought should be given to removing LIS programs from universities since library science might not be appropriate for teaching at the university level and developed in higher education largely as a result of Carnegie Corporation financial inducements;
- instead of a university-based approach, LIS education could return to the early twentieth-century model of ALA reviewing nondegree programs operating in major public libraries or other institutions;
- ALA itself might use distance education to administer such a program on the national level (Lee Shiflett to JESSE mailing list, March 2, 2007).

Shiflett is a leading library historian (Shiflett 2006), and he has done the library profession a significant service in bringing to a larger audience opinions concerning the future of library education that have been discussed, usually by information faculty and most often in private, since the rise to dominance of information science within ALA-accredited programs. Given the operation of academic freedom and the ability of faculty to raise unpopular questions, there is no reason whatsoever to believe that Shiflett himself endorses the expulsion of library education from the university in order to make intellectual room for the nonlibrary concerns of information-minded researchers. With this caveat noted, it is possible to point out that a number of his assertions make sense only if one views the North American library community as a passive entity, unwilling or unable to do what is necessary to defend or restore appropriate professional library education within public universities.

If properly understood and communicated, the professional nature of librarianship and its ability to help solve pressing American and Canadian problems is actually a plus for its longevity in North American higher education. Without going into excessive historical detail, it will be noted that universities in both medieval Europe and colonial America did not come into existence in order to provide faculty members with secure environments in which to conduct their research. These institutions were founded to deliver the education seen by their supporting cultures as necessary to solve their most pressing problems. In medieval Europe, the founding of a university often reflected a culture's need for educated physicians and church administrators. In seventeenth-century Massachusetts the present Harvard University was created not to advance theory but as a means of avoiding eternal damnation through assuring the availability of an educated clergy in the New England colonies (Previte-Orton 1952; Rudolph 1962/1990).

As was noted in Chapter 2, the early twenty-first century is a time when a remarkable number of the university's academic fields and disciplines seem to be developing their own "informatics" programs in order to carve out a piece of the lucrative information market. Consequently, the early twenty-first-century emphasis of ALA-accredited master's degree programs on information issues is seldom accorded priority of place within the university. LIS programs do not "own" the area of information education and research. More problematically, the futile attempts of such programs to achieve information eminence have distracted the American and Canadian library communities from emphasizing their potentially vital roles in helping to solve national learning, including reading, problems. This erroneous prioritizing of information in library education—as opposed to the undoubted priority of information within the "other" field of information science— has also muddied the message of library relevance in an information self-service age.

Prioritizing information provision over learning/reading facilitation in the education of academic, public, and school librarians has several short-term benefits for information educators. First, it allows their programs to offer inappropriate "one size fits all" courses and degrees. Unfortunately, it also has a distinctly negative impact on the professional lives of practitioners; it reinforces the inevitable cognitive dissonance afflicting those seeking to apply information theories to librarian realities. Second, having been taught to think only in information terms members of the library community have no intellectual basis for pressuring ALA-accredited programs to (a) restore or preserve the professional preparation necessary to meet critical public learning and reading needs, and (b) thereby secure the future of the professional librarian. Adopting the mindset that the fundamental role of libraries is information provision leads librarians and library supporters into the cardinal political and marketing sin of "getting off message." This problematic concentration on an information mediation role in the era of information self-service prevents them from justifying the library's relevance to what the public views as truly significant social problems. To borrow the pungent words of a British leader (or her speechwriter), for librarians to emphasize information over learning represents the destructive embrace of "yesterday's future" (Thatcher 1992).

The library community's misplaced loyalty to transformed professional education programs, based on an understandable emotional commitment to one's alma mater and a presumed mutuality of interest with LIS educators, militates against going public with disputes "within the family." This later situation seems to be in the process of changing since the lack of a shared culture between LIS professors and American and Canadian practitioners is becoming increasingly evident. Over time, a diffusing understanding that "library" and "information" actually do stand for separate, if equally commendable, co-cultures may be creating a distancing effect that can undermine the self-imposed restraint that academic, public, and school librarians have placed on themselves against using political and other pressure to reform errant ALA-accredited programs. In Chapter 3 the author addressed how public and legislative frustration with the extreme self-interest of Ohio's public universities left them open to "correction" by state government. The potential impact that outraged public opinion and concerned state legislatures can have on academic programs should not be underestimated by faculty. Information-oriented researchers who forget that libraries are often popular choices for solving public problems need to take to heart Gary Walker's reminder that, fundamentally, the "political culture is not an idea culture; it is a problem solving culture" and "leaders want solutions" (MacArthur Research Network 2005, 18). It remains the case that libraries and professional librarians more often provide such solutions than information educators do.

It should be noted the that the pessimistic views concerning professional library preparation at the university level that were brought to a larger audience through Shiflett's initial posting are not unique in the LIS literature. Over the years, a number of educators in LIS seem to have become more resistant to accepting the worth of a professional library education with a practical component. Blaise Cronin, dean of the ALA-accredited program at Indiana University, has asserted "there is pretty solid academic justification for spinning off librarianship programs from the major research universities and locating them in vocational education institutions" (Cronin 1995a, 57). In the end, such an effort may be self-defeating. Contemporary academic contexts are often driven by the need for cost containment and universities may see the considerable overlap between the "information" component of LIS and the field of communication or communication/media as an invitation to go beyond mere administrative realignment to truly merge programs and reduce costs by cutting the number of faculty lines. In consequence, moves by information educators to eliminate the library component from their graduate education may play out in the end as a fatal weakening of any justification for considering information science as anything other than a subset of the communication field.

The fact remains that in recent years a number of LIS programs have merged with schools of communication and schools of education (Hildreth and Koenig 2002). The value to librarianship of affiliating with programs of education will be considered in more detail in Chapter 5. Mergers of LIS schools into communication/media programs may reflect the possibility that the information-heavy rhetoric of both fields has convinced a significant number of senior university administrators that there exists more than a passing similarity in their missions. Although both fields support separate literatures, such artificial boundaries may not be the best defense against financial imperatives. It is now the case that communication researchers are cooperating with their Online Computer Library Center (OCLC) counterparts, using federal "library" dollars, and involving public and academic librarians in a project to bridge disciplinary boundaries (Dervin and Reinhard 2006). A few more such projects may even produce additional rationales for program mergers and higher education cost containment. It is inevitably dangerous for faculty careers and program longevity when either or both internal and external university funding sources identify extensive overlap and presidents and provosts want to raise the rate of return on the investment of academic dollars.

Arguments by information educators to expel library education from their public university programs suggest an inappropriately narrow understanding of the continuing lessons to be learned within North America regarding matters acceptable for teaching within the higher education world. Even with the spate of closings of

ALA-accredited programs in the late twentieth century, such assertions of the need to eliminate education for librarianship within higher education, particularly in public universities, may be seen as lacking adequate financial, historical, philosophical, and, most meaningfully, political underpinnings within American culture. The key variable for program survival is and has been the necessity for sufficient "feedback mechanisms" to insure that a program, in this case a program that purports to adequately educate librarians, meets the needs of significant constituencies that are capable of influencing university policies (Koenig 1990).

Theoretically, there is an enormous range of practical subjects where university-level instruction can be justified provided the faculty members involved take the necessary pains to insure that their instruction meets higher education's standards. In the oft-quoted words of Charles W. Eliot, the visionary academic who would become Harvard University's longest serving and most famous president, "It cannot be said too loudly or too often, that no subject of human inquiry can be out of place in the programme of a real university. It is only necessary that every subject should be taught at the university on a higher plane than elsewhere" (1869, 215–216). Such a claim of a place for educational relevance to the concerns of the mundane world has long been accepted by many on either side of the "preserving the best of the past" versus "adapting for the future" divide that often arises within higher education. This being the case, the reader might well wonder what would be the results for professional librarianship if the library community permits the "information-only" philosophy to extend its dominance within ALA-accredited programs to the point where it can and does expel appropriate library education from the university environment. Unfortunately, an example of such a negative transformation is already underway within the United Kingdom.

EXILING LIBRARY EDUCATION FROM THE UNIVERSITY: THE U.K. EXPERIENCE

As has already been discussed, much of contemporary North American information science is grounded in the claim that all librarians form a component of the information profession and function primarily as purveyors of information (Gorman 1999). This assertion of the meta-relevance of information for all things "library" was underscored for North American librarians in 2005 by Bob McKee, chief executive of the U.K. Chartered Institute of Library and Information Professionals (CILIP). Writing in the Canadian Library Association's popular journal *Feliciter* regarding the "success" of the April 1, 2002, merger of the U.K. Library Association and the Institute of Information Scientists that bought CILIP into being, McKee asserted, "convergence is the key for our profession in the information age" and claimed that "the roles and skills of librarians and information scientists and knowledge managers converge into a single set of core competencies" (2005, 72). Based on these premises, McKee went on to declare, "it makes sense for library and information professionals to recognize that they share a single professional domain—broadly based and containing distinct specialisms, but just as coherent a professional domain as engineering or medicine or teaching or the law" (72).

It is worth pointing out that McKee proclaimed the equation of information with library at the same time that the problems of U.K. librarianship identified in Chapter 2—abandonment of youth librarianship education, retreat from public library education, and repudiation of librarian expertise by university administrators—were gaining momentum. The obscuring or total avoidance of such negatives in McKee's laudatory account of the creation of CILIP, which may actually represent the further subjugation of library interests to information dominance, requires a certain caution in analysis. The author cannot but conclude that McKee's remarks to his Canadian readers suggests Howard S. Becker's earlier-cited formulation regarding the tendency of people who run organizations to smooth over "rough spots," hide "troubles," and deny "the existence of problems" (1998, 91). Setting aside the temptation to issue a more specific judgment as verging on an ad hominem argument it is nevertheless useful to examine several aspects of the remarkably medieval (by North American standards) response by CILIP to the widespread abandonment of librarianship by information educators.

First, CILIP seems to have set aside the possibility of fighting the progressive exiling of relevant library coursework from British universities in the political arena. To a certain extent the apparent unwillingness of practicing librarians to share accounts of their educational mistreatment by information educators in order to seek a more positive outcome with higher level university administrators, members of the general public, and powerful political leaders is reflective of a similar North American reticence about going public with such disputes.

As will be seen in Chapter 6 it may be necessary to overcome such er-roneous conceptions of solidarity in order to safeguard the future of professional librarianship in the North American context and thereby prevent a repetition of the U.K. retreat into an apprenticeship-like li-brary education. Attempting to hide or minimize the magnitude of the problems caused by the misapplication of otherwise legitimate in-formation science understandings to the education of professional li-brarians serves to cut off a significant source of support for library and librarian interests. It inevitably results in information "wins" and li-brary "losses" since higher education's information faculty are simply better than library practitioners at manipulating the operations of the internal academic system.

Since at least the middle of the last century, the American library community has grown very good at winning political fights when its aims correspond with public and legislative priorities. Even the most elite state universities can be influenced through a well-orchestrated political effort to support educating librarians to meet public needs when such an effort is grounded in demonstrations of how library ser-vices help solve critical social problems. CILIP's formal retreat into a guild-like approach to educating librarians (below) may be acceptable within the British hierarchical system. In North America it would be anathema to those who, in the words of the Canadian researcher Cynthia Hardy,

> Recognize that the conflicts experienced in the arena of higher edu-cation are not the result of miscommunication or misunderstand-ing, nor are they caused by aberrant individuals. They are the inevi-table result of the presence of different groups which, while working under the same broad paradigm, often have incompatible goals. It is perhaps not a very attractive framework; we are often reluctant to acknowledge such inherent tensions within our society. (Hardy 1996, 203)

The "incompatible goals" of professional librarians and informa-tion educators are becoming increasingly evident within the United Kingdom. It is instructive that British politicians, specifically mem-bers of the House of Commons, seem to have a greater recognition of the importance of libraries and librarians than do the professors of information management who are now in the process of expelling ap-propriate education from the U.K. higher education system. How else could one explain the remark of Sir Gerald Kaufman while chairing a

November 30, 2004, hearing on public libraries by the House of Commons Culture Media and Sport Committee? In the midst of the hearing Sir Gerald demanded that CILIP's Bob McKee join him and lie "down in the streets and blockade the libraries if any attempt is made to rename them 'resource centers' or anything like that" (Great Britain 2005, Ev 41). It is a "Marketing 101" premise that names with such a powerful resonance constitute "brands" that need to be enhanced and are not casual perceptions to be easily discarded without significant consequences (*Perceptions of Libraries and Information Resources* 2005).

Second, in lieu of bringing its fight for an appropriate education to the British public and political leadership, CILIP is reverting to a version of the medieval English craft system to develop future librarian expertise. In practice, it represents a returns to the early years of British professional librarianship when the dearth of educational opportunities in the United Kingdom resulted in efforts to raise professional standards through a guild-like structure operated by the former Library Association (founded 1877), one of the predecessor organizations to CILIP. It is an approach that is best explained to North American readers as something like the apprentice-journeyman-master (AJM) system that is yet found in contemporary trade and other unions. The critical importance of this retreat should not be underestimated. For a time it did appear that the British library community was joining the international movement to provide foundational education for librarianship within institutions of higher education. This sense of progress was lost in the educational crisis that came to a head in the early twenty-first century, when an antique structure that had seemingly become more of a means of formally recognizing achievement in the library and information worlds once again became critical for imparting basic instruction in professional librarianship.

The mechanics of the CILIP educational devolution involve endorsement of a process whereby the standard route recommended for advancement within librarian professional ranks now requires only a combination of work experiences, personal statements and development plans, mentoring, workshops, portfolios, and the like, all appropriately reviewed by relevant association boards and panels. As outlined, it appears to be the case that the new scheme allows a library employee with CILIP membership to rise from certified affiliate status as a paraprofessional to the higher ranks of "chartership" and, ultimately, "fellowship" *without earning any type of university degree* (CILIP 2004b, 6, see also 2004a).

Given the historic connection of the AJM occupational ladder with the manual trades in North American contexts, as well as Canadian and American preferences for associating professional preparation with higher education, any attempts to replace library education from an ALA-accredited university program with a CILIP-like association-based model would be controversial. It might be acceptable, if ratified by state-level regulations, in the rural areas and small towns that have always experienced difficulty in attracting professional librarians. However, it would be bitterly resented in many urban and suburban contexts. North American librarians already must fight formal suggestions that less-educated practitioners, some possessing only a high school diploma, ought to be accepted as full professional colleagues (Helmick and Swigger 2006, 62). Such claims are being advanced even at a time where the once legitimate excuse offered by those lacking professional education—being too distant from a source of higher education—is challenged by the availability of accredited undergraduate and graduate degrees via the Web. In the new environment of Internet-facilitated instruction, professionally educated librarians understand that a retreat from a university-based foundation for their field equates with deprofessionalization, reduced income, and the provision of minimal services "on the cheap."

The era of Abraham Lincoln is long over, and aspiring lawyers no longer "read law" under experienced attorneys as an acceptable professional preparation. Would-be physicians have long ceased learning their "trade" by convincing practicing doctors to take them on as an apprentice. Professional librarian tradition sees the creation of most ALA-accredited programs in state or provincial universities as the result of the extended efforts of academic, public, and school librarians, as well as and state and provincial library agencies—with or without the Carnegie Corporation funding noted by Shiflett. These yet influential sectors are well aware of the already noted reality that non-LIS sources for information-related education are springing up throughout the disciplines and fields of public universities and even community colleges. "Informatics" is clearly in academic fashion. Accordingly, formal proposals by information educators to disassociate librarian education from their schools or departments and replace such programs with the process of state certification or a CILIP-like association process could result in some unwanted education on political realties for those advocating such changes. Higher education administrators share numerous professional networks throughout North

America. Provosts, presidents, and rectors are aware of the effects of adverse publicity on their programs and fundraising activities. Accounts of academic leaders being grilled by a legislative committee over a proposal to abandon appropriate library education and well-publicized appearances by librarians and library supporters before higher education coordinating bodies or boards of trustees would spread remarkably fast in the Internet age. It would only take one or two such incidents to remind university heads about just how power-ful the combination of public sentiments and political realities can be in support of a library community that has earned state- or province-wide trust for its effectiveness in helping to solve critical problems.

Given the not-very-well-concealed desire of some information edu-cators to remove the "distraction" of providing a relevant library edu-cation from their programs, it is useful to examine the operation of the dominant information culture within ALA-accredited graduate education.

Exploring The Information Science Culture

A Matter of Definition

The long tradition of defining "information science" and disputing the resulting definitions (Rayward 1996) means that any formulation offered by the author is also subject to criticism. The primary focus of this work involves maintaining and extending the professionalism of librarianship in both its educational and practitioner contexts, even in the face of the regulatory capture of ALA accreditation by "informa-tion" supporters. In consequence, the author will use the definition of library and information studies adopted by ALA with the two men-tions of "library" deleted.

> The phrase "library and information studies" is understood to be concerned with recordable information and knowledge and the ser-vices and technologies to facilitate their management and use. Library and information studies encompasses information and knowledge creation, communication, identification, selection, acqui-sition, organization and description, storage and retrieval, preserva-tion, analysis, interpretation, evaluation, synthesis, dissemination, and management.
> (American Library Association 1992, 2)

Thus edited, ALA's definition of the field of library and information studies reveals what it really is—an information-centric formulation that ignores the historic and better founded education and learning roles of libraries. It is not much of an intellectual stretch to assert that the amended text forms a working definition of "information science" that could be included with so many of the other contested descriptions of the field (Dervin and Reinhard 2006).

Information Science as "Not Library"

A number of years ago the author attended a presentation at the annual conference of ALISE delivered by Blaise Cronin of Indiana. In a variation of his usual anti-library remarks, Cronin identified a "gulf between the two cultures" that "is no longer bridgeable" and asserted that only information science, not librarianship, was suitable for teaching and researching at the university level (Cronin 1995b, 897). On exiting the room, the author was behind two other conference attendees who were discussing the just completed presentation. One asked the other if she knew how Cronin defined "information science."

"That's easy," replied the other. "He defines it as 'not library.'"

In a presentation to the 2000's 66th IFLA (International Federation of Library Associations and Institutions) Council and General Conference, Ken Haycock of the University of British Columbia School of Library, Archival and Information Studies, summarized the information-versus-library problem as follows:

> In the period since 1992, the problems related to the graduate education of professional librarians, whether real or imagined, came to pervade professional and academic discourse and literatures. These were identified by the ALA Council, and others, as the growing elimination of the "L" word [library] from the names of schools, the seeming lack of attention to core competencies, with cataloguing often mentioned, and the national shortage in North America of professionals to work with particular groups, such as young people and disadvantaged populations in public libraries, and in particular environments, such as schools. (2 of 12)

While Haycock aptly provides a number of details, they can and should be considered symptoms directly related to the substitution of the corporate-research information paradigm for the academic, public, and school library-learning model in so many aspects of ALA-accredited education.

Theorizing About Information

The Nature of the Problem

The particulars—journalism's traditional who, what, when, where, why, and how—of the process through which the movement variously termed information science/information studies/information came to control professional education within ALA-accredited programs of North America are open to debate (Bates 2004). In an illuminative study of the development of information science at the University of Pittsburgh, William Aspray, a historian of science, identified "three separate traditions, each of which has been important in the rise of IS: library science, automated retrieval systems for scientific information, and military command-and-control systems" (1999, 4). These three intellectual streams may not have been present in all schools; indeed Aspray made it clear that "the field of information has many origins and its definition and practice are still widely open to debate" (17). It is of particular note that information does not require that its strongest connection be with library science or librarianship. On the level of a given university, information science is just as likely to have its closest affinity with computer science, cognitive science, communication, informatics, or engineering. Intellectual ancestry aside, the promotion of information science has almost inevitably carried with it a distinct tincture of "not library." Additionally, it is almost axiomatic that an information program within North America or the United Kingdom, even one claiming to educate library practitioners, will frequently employ some faculty with an anti-library bias (Aspray 1999; Bowles 1999; Cronin 2002; Webber 2003). In the Pittsburgh case, a former associate department chair saw library science as an "albatross" around the neck of the school since "library science did not have high stature in the university, and businesses were not aware that people trained as librarians could be useful employees" (Aspray 1999, 17).

Selecting Models for Understanding

On occasion, the author has used print and electronic forums to raise questions regarding the negative impact on library practitioners of the dominance of the information paradigm within the misnamed field of "library and information studies" (see Crowley 1998, 1999;

Crowley and Brace 1999). There is a certain irony in the fact that the author did so after earning his doctorate, not in the field of library and information studies, but in the area of higher education, albeit with a dissertation on the research university library (Crowley 1995). It would be misleading to claim that the choice of another field for the author's doctoral studies was a protest against the information education that has replaced relevant library studies in so many Ph.D. programs. The reality was that personal circumstances kept the author in Ohio, a state lacking a Ph.D. in library and information studies.

The author acknowledges that his inability to study at the doctoral level under the dwindling number of "library" faculty, or the "information" faculty with a generous sensibility to library realities, did result in having to spend additional time becoming more knowledgeable about ongoing developments in the separate library and information fields. Nevertheless, there was compensating value in being educated in a doctoral program that did not subsume librarians under the rubric of "information professionals" and was flexible enough to allow the author to write a dissertation on the research university library. Conversely, having interviewed potential faculty candidates for nearly eleven years at Dominican University, the author is well aware of the deficiencies of an "information science" Ph.D. education without library experience. It can and often will develop in "information" scholars a palpable disdain for the issues facing academic, public, and school libraries. For such scholars, the prospect of engaging in the development of information theory, no matter how irrelevant such theory is to real world contexts, has clear pride of place.

In researching this present work, the author encountered a valuable theoretical tool unidentified with either the "library" or the "information" fields. In "A General Theory of Scientific/Intellectual Movements," appearing in the April 2005 issue of the *American Sociological Review*, Scott Frickel and Neil Gross offer an intellectual formulation that "seeks to answer the question, under what social conditions is any particular scientific/intellectual movement or SIM . . . most likely to emerge, gain adherents, win intellectual prestige, and ultimately acquire some level of institutional stability?" (205). When combined with the earlier noted concept of "regulatory capture," their formulation is particularly useful for analyzing the rise of information science within programs established to educate professional librarians.

What are scientific/intellectual movements or SIMs? According to Frickel and Gross, "the most abbreviated definition is this: SIMs are collective efforts to pursue research programs or projects for thought in the face of resistance from others in the scientific or intellectual community" (2005, 206). As will be discussed, the dominance achieved by "information" adherents over their "library" counterparts within ALA-accredited programs of library and information studies represents both program-level success and higher education and worldwide disappointment. Information researchers have gained control of many ALA-accredited programs and in a few instances have greatly expanded the size of their faculty. However, in the majority of cases they seem to have been outmaneuvered by competitors from other fields and disciplines in their efforts to achieve recognition for "information leadership" on their university campuses and in the global information economy.

The Capture of "Library" Education

In their larger definition of scientific/intellectual movements Frickel and Gross (2005) offer a number of assumptions concerning the nature of such forces. Drawing on the work of these theorists, it can be asserted that the scientific/intellectual movement known as information studies succeeded in its efforts to subordinate the field of library science and to dominate the interim field of library and information studies because the movement

1. had a rational program for achieving control;
2. persisted in promoting change against the resistance of many library practitioners and "library" educators;
3. understood that the process of change is inherently political and that the information movement needed to secure control over the academic units that supported education for librarianship, while simultaneously capturing the ALA accreditation structure;
4. attracted high-status and other scholars frustrated by decades of practitioner rejection of their theories by offering a "meta-paradigm"—information science—that did not require that its theories be relevant in off-campus environments. This attraction consisted of
   a. supporting opportunities for theory generation free of "library" practitioner influence;

    b. developing a close alignment with such information associations as American Society for Information Science and Technology (ASIS&T);

    c. organizing information conferences;

    d. determining what subjects of study are worthy of being funded and reported on in the leading journals and other publications of the field;

    e. socializing doctoral students into thinking, teaching, and researching along "information" instead of "library" models; and, most important,

    f. securing control over faculty appointments, particularly those in the ALA-accredited programs located in the more prestigious state universities, and recruiting faculty without library experience.

Since the above factors have an inevitable overlap they will be reviewed as a unified whole.

The Micro "Victory" and Macro "Defeat" of The Information Movement in ALA-Accredited Programs

Before discussing the associated outcomes whose achievement was fundamental to the information science agenda to establish academic legitimacy as a field in North America through, in part, transforming the library education provided in ALA-accredited programs, it is worth recalling that this transformation did not result from an unwanted intellectual invasion. *Information scholars were invited into the library education world.* Faculty members are usually appointed by the president, chancellor, or other head of an American or Canadian university after an extensive search process. In the early years of program transformation, information scholars were recommended for appointment to their positions by the "library" professors who were already employed teaching and researching in programs affiliated with the ALA accreditation system.

From an early twenty-first-century perspective, the first and most obvious outcome of this sustained effort was the capture and development of the necessary academic infrastructure, including faculty positions, grant dollars, research forums, publications, conferences, and related venues for bringing the results information investigations and/or theorizing to a larger academic and practitioner audience. This primary goal involved the secondary yet critical aims of (1) severing or minimizing the traditional connection of "librarianship" from/with the field of education during the transformation from "library" to "information" education, and (2) gaining a greater level of recognition and enhanced prestige within the academic world than had been achieved by their "library" education predecessors. Although this agenda, achieved only in part, was ambitious, information educators were not the first to argue in favor of repositioning librarianship away from education.

In the 1950 work *The Public Library in the United States,* political scientist Robert D. Leigh, director of the massive study termed the *Public Library Inquiry,* argued against the tendency of mid-twentieth-century librarians to "conceive of themselves as performing an educational task" (25). Instead, Leigh asserted that supporters of the public library would be better off envisioning it as "an agency of communication" (26). The importance of Leigh's arguments lies in the fact that it is possible to see the field of communication as either the "original" information field or at least a sister field that developed contemporaneously with what is now termed "information studies." This mutuality of interests, amounting to coalescence, is discernable through a close reading of Leigh's extended 1950 arguments for embedding "library" in the field of communication. The overlap with information is such that Leigh's points, with adjustments for technological enhancements over nearly six decades, are echoed in contemporary arguments that librarianship is quintessentially a part of the field of "information studies" (Bates 1999). One simply has to substitute "information revolution" for the half-century old "communications revolution" (Leigh 1950, 26) and the anti-education "script" can and does play out with a certain amount of déjà-vu.

Both Leigh's advocacy for subsuming library and librarian under communication and the "rational program" developed by the information theorists to achieve control within ALA-accredited departments and schools are attempts to deny the historic connection between librarianship and education. Each would try to rebut Harold Lancour's 1948 claim that "there has been, throughout the years, a growing awareness that the discipline to which librarianship is most closely allied is the field of education" (1949/1971, 64). In addition, they would likely reject out of hand Lancour's additional argument in support of the "the conscious recognition that all libraries are educational institutions and, by analogy, that all librarians are educators" (64). As will be discussed in the next chapter, Lancour's decades-old assertions remain valid for academic, public, and school libraries.

In addition to the obvious reason that information concerns are not totally identifiable with education issues, the movement by information educators to divorce librarianship from education, even as they attempt to bury the former so far under information science that it is no longer identifiable, may reflect more problematic causes. It suggests a move by information educators to distance themselves from the campus librarians who, ironically, may be graduates of their own programs.

Unlike the yearly Canadian university rankings published in *Maclean's*, the American equivalents appearing in the *U.S. News and World Report*, or even the more research-oriented analyses of status within fields and disciplines across the academic world (Becher 1989; Clark 1987), studies involving prestige on a given campus (Cuban 1999) are relatively rare. In one such consideration, after the inevitable priority listings of university officials, professors of medicine, law, and physics topped the university status listing for teaching and research faculty. The lowest ranked faculty class was "assistant professor of education." Situated even lower on the list was "librarian," a category that outranked a "counselor, student counseling center" but fell one notch below "assistant football coach" (Wolfle 1983, 460–461).

The fear of information faculty that the "library taint" may produce low academic status is sometimes accompanied by anxiety over being confused by campus colleagues with the people working in the university library. It can also reflect faculty concern over returning to the days when practitioners seeking pertinent instruction and resenting "irrelevant" theory (O'Connor and Mulvaney 1996) seemed to dominate the ALA accreditation process. It could even be a mixture of these and other causes. Whatever the case, the resulting gumbo of motivations can induce information scholars to signal their independence from practitioners through removing the word "library" from the name of their ALA-accredited program. In this context it is well to recall that both the provost who closed Columbia University's famed School of Library Service and the review committee that studied and recommended on its future prospects saw the name "library" as being a negative for recruiting faculty from the ranks of the information research elite (Cole 1990, 29).

The "rational program" that resulted in the success of the information movement within ALA-accredited programs can be summarized succinctly:

- secure the appointment of "information" over "library" faculty and thereby obtain control of the ALA-accredited program;
- argue that "information" is more research friendly than "library";
- drop the word "library" from the name of the program; and finally,
- emphasize information research and teaching over their library equivalents until the growth in the number of "information" students allows the exiling of "library education" and would-be librarians from one's program if their demands for instructional relevance are determined by information faculty to have become too onerous (King 2005, 15).

The success of the "micro" information program to capture departments and schools offering ALA-accredited degrees is particularly notable in light of the failure of the information science "macro" program to achieve similar successes on the campus and in the wider community. Even within the subfield of ALA-accredited programs, the dismantling of the informatics program located in the University at Buffalo (Lorna Peterson to JESSE mailing list, February 22, 2007) may represent a negative intellectual milestone for the pretensions of information researchers (Cochrane 2006). Of far more importance on the macro level of universities and the global economy may be the attempt to redefine the "field" of information away from something like an irresistible intellectual force able to prescribe "information rules' to other fields and disciplines. Of late, ALA-accredited and other "information" programs unconnected to a "content" field or discipline seem have gone in search not of followers but of allies and are seeking connections with scholars researching information assistance from more traditional bases in the humanities, social sciences, and sciences (Harmon 2006a, 2006b).

Such disciplinary modesty is welcome. It is also likely to enhance the prospects for collaborative information-related research. However, there remains the fact that in the new era of Google and social networking, information theory does not provide a sound basis for sustaining library professionalism or even for assuring the future of the library.

HOPE FOR THE FUTURE OF LIBRARY EDUCATION

For both aspiring and long-established librarians, as well as advocates for library services within geographic, academic, and school communities, this chapter's discussion of the dominance of "information" over "library" in the captured ALA system of accreditation ought to be a source of concern regarding relevant professional education. The triumph of the field of information over the distinctly different field of librarianship is a fascinating phenomenon for those, like the author, who have a Ph.D. in higher education and an interest in studying academic change, no matter how negative it may be. The current situation involves a tension that cannot endure over time. Information science is simply not librarianship. Its temporary domination of things library may well be the "episodic"—and thus transitory—phenomenon described by Frickel and Gross (2005, 208). Left unchecked, it is also possible that North America will follow the precedent of the United Kingdom and information will ultimately eject librarianship from the very programs that librarians brought into being. Alternatively, a revived library model whose supporters are unafraid of wielding political and higher education power can negotiate with information science to insure that ALA-accredited programs are educating for library realities.

REFERENCES

American Library Association. 1992. *Standards for Accreditation of Master's Programs in Library & Information Studies*. Chicago: Office for Accreditation, American Library Association.

Argyris, Chris. 1999. Tacit knowledge and management. In *Tacit Knowledge in Professional Practice: Researcher and Practitioner Perspectives,* ed. Robert J. Sternberg and Joseph A. Horvath, 123–140. Mahwah, NJ: Lawrence Erlbaum Associates.

Aspray, William. 1999. Command and control, documentation, and library science: The origins of information science at the University of Pittsburgh. *IEEE Annals of the History of Computing* 21, no. 4 (October–December): 4–20.

Bates, Marcia J. 1999. The invisible substrate of information science. *Journal of the American Society for Information Science* 50, no. 12 (October): 1043–1050.

———. 2004. Information science at the University of California at Berkeley in the 1960s: A memoir of student days. *Library Trends* 52, no. 4 (spring): 683–701.

Becher, Tony. 1989. *Academic Tribes and Territories: Intellectual Enquiry And The Cultures of Disciplines*. Buckingham, England: Society for Research into Higher Education and Open University Press.

Becker, Howard S. 1998. *Tricks of the Trade: How to Think About Your Research While You're Doing It.* Chicago: University of Chicago Press.

Bowles, Mark D. 1999. The information wars: Two cultures and the conflict in information retrieval, 1945–1999. in *Proceedings of the 1998 Conference on the History and Heritage of Science Information Systems,* ed. Mary Ellen Bowen, Trudi Bellardo Hahn, Robert V. Williams, 156–166. Medford, NJ: Published for the American Society for Information Science and the Chemical Heritage Foundation by Information Today.

Chartered Institute of Library and Information Professionals (CILIP). 2004a. *Body of Professional Knowledge: Setting Out an Adaptable and Flexible Framework for Your Changing Needs.* London: Chartered Institute of Library and Information Professionals. http://www.cilip.org.uk/qualificationschartership/bpk (accessed March 7, 2007).

———. 2004b. *Certification Scheme Handbook: CILIP's Framework of Qualifications, Enhancing Opportunities, Rewarding Achievement.* London: Chartered Institute of Library and Information Professionals. http://www.cilip.org.uk/qualification-schartership/ FrameworkofQualifications/certification (accessed March 7, 2007).

Clark, Burton R. 1987. *The Academic Life: Small Worlds, Different Worlds.* Princeton, NJ: Carnegie Foundation for the Advancement of Teaching.

Cochrane, Mary. 2006. FSEC supports dissolving informatics school. *University at Buffalo Reporter,* November 30, 2006. http://www.buffalo.edu/reporter/vol38/vol38n13/articles/FSEC.html (accessed April 2, 2007).

Cole, Jonathan R. 1990. *Report of the Provost on the School of Library Service at Columbia.* New York: Columbia University in the City of New York.

Cronin, Blaise. 1995a. Shibboleth and substance in North American library and information science education. *Libri* 45, no. 1 (March): 45–63.

———. 1995b. Cutting the Gordian knot. *Information Processing & Management* 31, no. 6 (November): 897–902.

———. 2002. Holding the center while prospecting at the periphery: Domain identity and coherence in North American information studies education. *Education for Information* 20, no. 1 (March): 3–10.

Crowley, Bill. 1998. Dumping the "Library." *Library Journal,* 120 (July): 48–49.

———. 1999. The control and direction of professional education. *Journal of the American Society for Information Science* 50, no. 12 (October): 1127–1135.

Crowley, Bill, and Bill Brace. 1999. A choice of futures: Is it libraries versus information? *American Libraries* 30 (April): 76–77, 79.

Crowley, William A. Jr. 1995. A Draft Research Model of the Research University Library: Exploring the Scholar-Librarian Partnership of Jaroslav Pelikan in *The Idea of the University: A Reexamination.* PhD. diss., Ohio University, 1995.

Cuban, Larry. 1999. *How Scholars Trumped Teachers: Change Without Reform in University Curriculum, Teaching, and Research, 1890–1990.* New York: Teachers College Press.

Dervin, Brenda, and CarrieLynn D. Reinhard. 2006. Researchers and practitioners talk about users and each other. Making user and audience studies

matter—paper 1. *Information Research* 12, no 1. (October). http://informationr
.net/ir/12-1/paper286.html (accessed March 8, 2007).

Eliot, Charles W. 1869. "The new education, parts 1 and 2." *Atlantic Monthly* 23:
203–220, 356–367.

Frickel, Scott, and Neil Gross. 2005. A general theory of scientific/intellectual
movements. *American Sociological Review* 70, no. 2 (April): 204–232.

Gorman, G. E. 1999. The future for library science education. *Libri* 49, no. 1
(March): 1–10.

Gorman, Michael. 2004. Whither library education? *New Library World* 105, nos.
1204/1205 (September): 376–380.

Great Britain. Parliament. House of Commons. Culture, Media and Sport
Committee. 2005. *Public Libraries.* Vol. 2. London: Stationary Office. http://
www.publications.parliament.uk/pa/cm200405/cmselect/cmcumeds/81/81i
.pdf (accessed January 27, 2007).

Hardy, Cynthia. 1996. *The Politics of Collegiality: Retrenchment Strategies in Canadian
Universities.* Montreal & Kingston: McGill-Queen's University Press.

Harmon, Glynn, ed. 2006a. Introduction. The first I-conference of the I-school
communities. Special section, *Bulletin of the American Society for Information
Science and Technology* (April/May): 9–10.

——. ed. 2006b. The first I-Conference of the I-school communities. Special section, *Bulletin of the American Society for Information Science and Technology* (April/
May): 9–23.

Haycock, Ken. 2000. The congress on professional education in North America.
Paper presented at the 66th IFLA Council and General Conference, Jerusalem,
Israel. http://www.ifla.org/IV/ifla66/papers/146-156e.htm (accessed March 29,
2007).

Helmick, Catherine, and Keith Swigger. 2006. Core competencies of library practitioners. *Public Libraries* 45, no. 2 (March/April): 54–69.

Hildreth, Charles R., and Michael Koenig. 2002. Organizational realignment of
LIS programs in academia: From independent standalone units to incorporated programs. *Journal of Education for Library and Information Science* 43, no. 2
(spring): 126–133.

King, John Leslie. 2005. Stepping up: Shaping the future of the field. Presentation
at the annual meeting of the Association for Library and Information Science
Education January 14, 2005. Digital Library of Information Science and
Technology (dLIST). http://dlist.sir.arizona.edu/739 (accessed February 26,
2007).

Koenig, Michael E. D. 1990. Buttering the toast evenly: Library school closings at
Columbia and Chicago are tragic; but they don't have to signal a trend. *American
Libraries* 21 (September): 723–724, 726.

Lancour, Harold. 1949/1971. Discussion. In *Education for Librarianship: Papers
Presented at the Library Conference, University of Chicago, August 16–21, 1948,* ed.
Bernard Berelson, 59–65. Rpt. Freeport, NY: Books for Libraries Press.

Leigh, Robert D. 1950. *The Public Library in the United States.* New York: Columbia
University Press, 1950.

MacArthur Research Network on Transitions to Adulthood and Chapin Hall Center for Children at the University of Chicago. 2005. *Adolescence and the Transition to Adulthood: Rethinking Public Policy for a New Century.* Philadelphia: MacArthur Research Network on Transitions to Adulthood and University of Pennsylvania.

McKee, Bob. 2005. Futureproofing our professional association—convergence and CILIP. *Feliciter* 51 (2): 72–75.

O'Connor, Daniel, and J. Philip Mulvaney. 1996. LIS faculty research and expectations of the academic culture versus the needs of the practitioner. *Journal of Education for Library and Information Science* 37, no. 4 (fall): 306–316.

Perceptions of Libraries and Information Resources: A Report to the OCLC Membership. 2005. Principal contributors, Cathy De Rosa et al. Dublin, OH: OCLC Online Computer Library Center. http://www.oclc.org/reports/2005perceptions.htm (accessed September 22, 2006).

Previte-Orton, Charles W. 1952. *The Shorter Cambridge Medieval History.* Vol. 1. *The Later Roman Empire to the Twelfth Century.* Cambridge: Cambridge University Press.

Rayward, W. Boyd. 1996. The history and historiography of information science: Some reflections. *Information Processing & Management* 32, no. 1: 3–17.

Rudolph, Frederick. 1962/1990. *The American College and University: A History.* Repr. Athens: University of Georgia Press.

Shiflett, Lee. 2006. Biographical statement. Biographical Statements for Conference Speakers. Fifteenth North Carolina Serials Conference—Crystal Clear? Today's Libraries, Tomorrow's Library Users, March 30–31, 2006. http://www.nccuslis.org/conted/serials2006/serials2006bios.htm (accessed March 8, 2007).

Thatcher, Margaret. 1992. Speech in the Hague ("Europe's Political Architecture"). The Hague, Netherlands, May 15, 1992. http://www.margaretthatcher.org/speeches/displaydocument.asp?docid=108296 (accessed March 27, 2007).

Webber, Sheila. 2003. Information science in 2003: A critique. *Journal of Information Science* 29, no. 4 (July 1): 311–330.

Wolfle. Lee M. 1983. Prestige in American universities. *Research in Higher Education* 18, no. 4 (December): 455–472.

CHAPTER 5

The Ebbing of Information Science

PROFESSIONAL STATUS AND CATALOGING

Quite some time ago, when the author was working full-time at the New York Public Library and beginning part-time studies for a master's degree at the now-defunct Columbia University School of Library Service, he sat in the back of the room listening as a professor outlined the library status hierarchy. At the top of the class blackboard, the instructor placed academic libraries and special libraries (corporate, law, medical, etc.). At the bottom, he listed public libraries and school libraries. Stepping back to consider his work, he then drew a thick line across the blackboard, dividing the top from the bottom.

"The line in the middle of the blackboard is the status line," he explained. "Academic libraries, since they are associated with universities and colleges have a correspondingly high status. Medical, law, and corporate libraries, what we term special libraries because they are not easy to categorize, also have it."

The professor then frowned. "It is an unfortunate fact of life that public libraries and school libraries do not have much professional standing. While I disagree, there are even some in our field who view such libraries are where you work if you do not have what it takes for a successful career in the academic or corporate worlds."

After depressing all or most of the aspiring public and school librarians in the class, including the author, this professor then went on to describe how cataloging became the route through which librarianship gained a place in the academic world.

"In the late nineteenth and early twentieth centuries it was the librarian's ability to organize the massive collections needed to support scholarship across the fields and disciplines in the emerging research universities that became the theoretical basis of library science," the professor insisted. "Cataloging made librarianship a science and it supports our professional standing."

Decades ago, before the "friendly capture" of American Library Association-accredited library education programs by information advocates, many baby boomers and older librarians received similar lectures on both the prestige hierarchy within the library world and the fundamentally important value of cataloging in supporting librarianship's claim to be a profession. Given the contention that cataloging and the librarian's status were unalterably intertwined—no matter how technological developments would later undermine this correlation—it should surprise no one that many of today's long-established practitioners see the elimination of a required course in cataloging as a direct assault on their professional identities (Gorman 2004; Haycock 2000). This association may explain much of the negative professional reaction to an *Arizona Republic* report of May 30, 2007, describing how the new Perry Branch Library of the Maricopa County Library District would open in Gilbert, Arizona, with its collection organized on the topic and alphabetical order bookstore shelving model instead of the more complicated Dewey Decimal Classification (DDC) used in so many public libraries (Wingett 2007).

This Arizona plan to replace the DDC organization of a library collection with a retail-like approach generated quite a number of exchanges on Publib, an electronic discussion list maintained "for the discussion of issues relating to public librarianship" (Publib). Not all the comments on the topic were negative; some postings actually supported the abandonment of the DDC layout by the Perry Branch. This backing often reflected a commonsense understanding that in America's free enterprise culture it was only to be expected that for-profit bookstore chains would use a shelf arrangement that maximized sales and the profits to be made from readers, viewers, gamers, and the like.

Other Publib participants strongly disagreed, noting that the process of organizing material by DDC represented a more precise subject arrangement and was fundamentally important to the goal of making a library collection broadly accessible. As such it was also one of the positive ways that libraries can be distinguished from bookstores (*Publib Digest* 26, 39 [May 31, 2007]; *Publib Digest* 27, 3 [June 1, 2007]).

Here it is useful to point out that appreciation of effective cataloging can extend far beyond the boundaries of the occasionally overlapping library and information worlds. While this chapter was being written, the author discussed the value of cataloging with a brilliant professor emerita of medieval history, a woman with a restless intellect, who was comfortable with technology and who frequently disregarded disciplinary boundaries throughout her working life. Such qualities even led her to take the time to acquire master's degrees in both business and library science on a part-time basis after earning a doctorate from the University of Chicago and embarking on an extended career of research and teaching. Over coffee, this senior academic defended the value of descriptive cataloging, stressing how in her own class on the subject she had enjoyed the intellectual challenge of assessing library holdings and describing their contents so as to maximize the value of the intellectual resources involved for researching and teaching across a variety of the university's fields and disciplines.

"Then" Versus "Now"

Cataloging and Librarian Professionalism

The current era is a time when many library, information, and knowledge professionals with ALA-accredited master's degrees do little or no original cataloging. In recent decades, libraries have reduced costs and the number of professional catalogers by acquiring copy cataloging through the Online Computer Library Center (OCLC). Aside from the financial savings represented, this transformation has enormous symbolic importance; it signals the decreased value for individual libraries of the original cataloging that for so long was a mark of librarian professionalism. Coupled with the reality that end users are increasingly bypassing librarians and other library staff to access intellectual and other resources on the Internet through search engines and key words (*Perceptions of Libraries and Information Resources* 2005), the decline in original cataloging makes it clear that online catalogs represent only one possible tool among several for locating knowledge, information, and stories. For the first time in the histories of the separate library and information fields, it is now legitimate to question whether or not cataloging remains fundamental to the skill set of *every* professional educated in ALA-accredited programs, particularly those aspiring to careers in corporate and research contexts where the tools of practice increasingly consist of an office cubicle and accessible electronic resources.

Since vendors can and will make mistakes regarding the classification of hard-copy books, it remains a viable argument that academic, public, and school librarians will need a cataloging background, if only for quality control purposes, for as long as the paper monograph remains a viable format. Nevertheless, even in libraries with collections where the value of original cataloging remains evident, it has been quite a long time since every professional librarian in every library had to be prepared to carry out such duties. The author, for example, during a twenty-three-year-long career involving a variety of positions in public, state, and multitype libraries, did not catalog a single work after completing the in-class and homework assignments for the required cataloging course at the former Columbia University School of Library Service.

The increased reliance of libraries on copy cataloging, coupled with the public's relentless embrace of electronic resources, has irreversibly weakened the equation of cataloging with the professionalism of every librarian, information specialist, and knowledge manager. Ironically, the concurrent and growing reliance of the public and the library and information professions on Web sites and, to a lesser extent, full-text databases seems to have enhanced the value of the library and librarian's roles in facilitating lifelong learning. Instruction and learning are now seemingly ever-present in the library—as opposed to the information—world. The metaphorical wheel of a librarian's professional responsibilities seems to have fully turned. As will be recalled, the roles of the librarian and library as learning facilitators were deemed to be of fundamental importance in the early years of the American library movement (*Upon the Objects to be Attained* 1852). The learning role of libraries still resonates with the public at large and doubtlessly influenced the decision of the Cleveland Public Library to term itself "'The People's University' on all its print materials and its web site" (Fialkoff 2007, 8).

Information and Mythic Fact—Again

In Chapter 2 the claim that "library" can be realistically subsumed under "information" was explored as an example of the mixed truth and fable approach to scholarship described by the term "mythic fact" (Crowley 1999; Maines, Bridger, and Ulmer 1996). The negative effects of embracing this information model are such that they deserve a more extended consideration. Drawing on the both classical sociological theory (Mead [1932]/1959, 166) and more recent elaborations (Maines, Bridger, and Ulmer 1996, 536) it is possible to see theories attempting to sever academic, public, and school libraries and librarians from their essential connections with learning and redefine them as mere "information intermediaries" represent fundamental errors. Such theories are major "mythic facts" that constitute "collective delusions with the power to set scholarly agendas" (Maines, Bridger, and Ulmer 1996, 536). While library as information intermediary theoretical approaches may have had the short-term effect of strengthening the position of some information theorists in some aspects of the academic world, they consistently fail to provide a vision of the library that is valued in the larger North American academic and civic cultures. One need to look no further than the realignment of a growing number of ALA-accredited information programs, not as university information leaders but as subordinate components of other academic units (Hildreth and Koenig 2002; Koenig and Hildreth 2002). This development has demonstrated that the same "mythic facts" regarding information that seem to be so persuasive to faculty members within many ALA-accredited programs can appear as merely professorial wishful thinking to academic administrators with university-wide responsibilities.

Within the ill-defined range of mythic facts promulgated about the library and librarian's subordinate roles in the larger information environment are two fundamental assertions

1. Information is becoming the source of future growth in the globalized economy. This process will lead to the recognition by universities and the larger world that those ALA-accredited programs transformed from "library" to "information" are a critically important source of relevant expertise. In consequence, the ranks of information faculty will grow and such faculty will receive enhanced compensation, more prestige, increased influence in campus and public forums, and, in consequence, improved job security.
2. This recognition of the leadership role of information science and its faculty will increase the career prospects of practitioners who graduate from schools of information offering ALA-accredited and other degrees.

The author is a pragmatist and in *Spanning the Theory-Practice Divide in Library and Information Science* (Crowley 2005) he repeatedly emphasized the need to subject such broad theoretical claims to the test of analyzed experience. Any reasonable analysis will reveal that for librarianship the actions taken on the basis of assertions of unlimited benefits from adopting information science models have produced decidedly mixed results. Nevertheless, Mythic Fact #1, or the assumption that information is the primary source of growth in the globalized economy and that faculty will benefit from transforming ALA-accredited programs into information schools, has proven partially correct. Information is a huge sector of the economy in many advanced nations and the status of information professors has indeed improved at such institutions as Florida State University, the University of Michigan, and the University of Washington. However, the "mythic" aspect of "mythic fact" for this claim comes into play if one makes the mistake of assuming that a few successful information programs, in effect what statisticians see as misleading "outliers," actually represent the future of programs offering ALA-endorsed education for the separate library and information worlds. Unfortunately, this error will be seen to be repeatedly "in play" during this chapter's exploration of the reasons why information supporters achieved their dominance throughout much of the system of ALA-accredited education.

Mythic Fact #2, or the assumption that subsuming library under information is going to advance the career prospects of professional librarians, represents a truly problematic version of wishful thinking. It functions to blind many information scholars to the profoundly negative results of equating librarian with information producers at a time when the advances in information retrieval represented by Google and other search engines are perceived to be eliminating the need for and status of information intermediaries.

In Chapter 4 the author first drew on the theorizing of Scott Frickel and Neil Gross regarding the growth, flourishing, and decline of "scientific/intellectual movements" within the university world (2005). The intent was to provide the reader with an understanding of the process—the *how*—through which information came to dominate library within programs offering ALA-accredited master's degrees. This analysis of the progression of program transformation builds on several of the author's previous considerations of the topic (Crowley 1999; Crowley and Ginsberg 2003, 2005). More important, it draws from a substantial body of literature addressing fundamental intellectual change within academic and research fields and disciplines. In addition to the theorizing of Frickel and Gross (2005), this literature includes such important monographic works as Thomas S. Kuhn's *The Structure of Scientific Revolutions* (1970), Andrew Abbott's

The System of Professions: An Essay on the Division of Expert Labor (1988), and Larry Cuban's *How Scholars Trumped Teachers: Change Without Reform in University Curriculum, Teaching, and Research 1890-1990* (1999).

THE INFORMATION SCIENCE CAPTURE OF LIBRARY EDUCATION

A Self-Evident Truth?

Perhaps naively, the author will assume that informed readers, particularly those employed in academic contexts, are familiar with the reality that there are predictable patterns for how intellectual movements achieve ascendancy within university environments (Abbott 1988; Frickel and Gross 2005; Kuhn 1970). He also assumes that such readers will recognize that the present dominance of information over library within the ALA system of accredited professional education represents the success of just such a movement. The twenty-first-century reality that information dominates library within ALA-accredited programs is exemplified by such factors as the information movement's (a) control over the process of faculty recruitment and the education offered in doctoral programs, (b) success in deleting library from program names, and (c) ability to insure that information views are seldom seriously challenged via a textbook adoption process that guarantees a greater market share for works describing a subservient status of librarianship within the information model. A prominent example of such a textbook is Richard E. Rubin's widely used and well-written *Foundations of Library and Information Science* (2004).

It is to be expected that many readers who accept the reality of an information capture of library education programs, but who also are committed information advocates, will contest the author's analysis of the reasons *why* this process took place, as well as his perception that the results of the capture are and will increasingly be damaging for much of the library world. Given this probability, the author will stress the fact that recognizing the negatives of an information-centric education for librarians, as opposed to the undoubted value of such education for information specialists and knowledge managers, is not the same as claiming that this condition was actually intended by most of the information faculty involved. That most faculty information advocates mean well, are not maliciously opposed to librarianship, and regularly exhibit support for the careers of aspiring librarians is here stipulated. As will be seen, the negatives arising from the information capture of library education are systemic in nature and reflect the difficulties of applying information science concepts to the separate field of librarianship.

In his classic essay "The Professions Under Siege," Jacques Barzun identified three faults of higher education faculty that are "known" or "suspected" yet "hard to prove." Several of these shortcomings— "academic incompetence, indifference, misdirection of effort" (1978, 62) require a nuanced discussion of their relevance to library and information issues. Faculty information advocates and theorists, including those with a demonstrated sympathy for librarianship (Michael E. D. Koenig) and the relative few who openly view it with disdain (Blaise Cronin), have long numbered among the research "stars" of ALA-accredited programs. As information's "best and brightest," the intellectual capability of these and like-minded scholars has been demonstrated in numerous forums for quite a number of years.

Consequently, any valid bill of indictment for the unintended intellectual crime of undermining libraries and librarians must start with the relative indifference of many information scholars to the true concerns of librarianship. Often without substantial work experience in libraries or even information and knowledge management centers, and lacking degrees in the field, such faculty can easily subsume library matters under their own research interests. Ironically, one of the better explanations of the causes of this process was offered by Patrick Wilson, an influential teacher of many information theorists and advocates (Bates 2004, 695; Sue Easun, personal communication, 2000). Wilson provided an apt if inadvertent description of why information theorists cannot easily conceptualize for the library domain in his *Second-Hand Knowledge: An Inquiry into Cognitive Authority* when he observed that "theoretical lenses" can provide such inaccurate and distorted understandings of the world that "they lead one to think one is seeing things that are not there; and they prevent one from seeing things that are there" (1983, 6).

"Information," of course, is a theoretical lens and the "information bias error" can and often does obscure the reality that librarianship and information science have developed into quite different fields concerned with different societal problems. To again build on Barzun's theorizing" (1978, 62) the resulting *indifference* of a number of information science professors to understanding "library" on its own terms tends to result in the second part of the indictment, that information faculty exhibit a clear misdirection of effort away from the teaching and research necessary to enhancing the value of libraries and the worth of professional librarians.

It must be recognized that subsuming "library" as a subordinate part of the "information infrastructure" (Rubin 2004) tends to be a productive strategy for information scholars. Even in a time of growing end user self-service, this assignment of library to a status of secondary importance in former library schools is used to justify diverting to information concerns the income streams derived from student tuition and state subsidies intended to support librarian education. The resulting library-deficient, information-abundant professional instruction that is often present in ALA-accredited programs now provides future practitioners with little in the way of effective models for program and personal survival in contemporary academic, public, and school library contexts.

It is to be recalled that Chapter 3 was entitled "What's the story?"– the question at the heart of the Goldberg Rule advocated by Richard E. Neustadt and Ernest R. May in their *Thinking in Time: The Uses of History for Decision-Makers* (1986). Neustadt and May named the "rule" after the problem-solving approach taken by business executive Avram Goldberg, who asked his managers to provide him with the "story" behind the problems they wanted him to consider. When done correctly, this approach helps provide vital context for successful decision making since, for example, it leads analysts to accept the possibility that misleading matters might be concealing the true natures of the problem and its causes.

Two Types of "Whys"

This chapter will consider two types of whys related to information's performance within higher education. The first why is historical and addresses the factors that made possible the problematic dominance of information over library in programs accredited by ALA. The second why, one too little discussed, deals with the failure of information educators to extend such dominance and achieve recognition for information expertise in their larger campus environments. As the research of Charles Hildreth and Michael E. D. Koenig has demonstrated, the actions of the university world, with a few notable exceptions, seem to demonstrate more of a dismissal of the claims of faculty members in ALA-accredited programs to campus information leadership and less of a willingness to provide the funding and faculty lines to turn such aspirations into reality. In the twenty-first century, an "information program" offering an ALA-accredited degree in a major university is less likely to become a stand-alone campus luminary than to be assigned a subordinate position within a school of "communications-media" or "education" (Hildreth and Koenig 2002; Koenig and Hildreth 2002).

In Chapters 3 and 4 it was emphasized that the information researchers who eventually came to dominate library education were invited to take teaching and research positions within ALA-accredited programs. The resulting transformation of such programs in a direction that minimized library concerns in favor of maximizing information prospects was a decades long effort, aptly symbolized by the 2000 report of the W. K. Kellogg Foundation–supported KALIPER project (the Kellogg-ALISE Information Professions Education Renewal). Setting aside its self-justifying rhetoric, it can be seen that the KALIPER effort—led by several major university programs—openly proclaimed its intention to subordinate and thereby marginalize "library" under "information" within both individual universities and the overall system of ALA accreditation (KALIPER 2000). For many of the faculty involved, the demotion of librarianship was justified by the burgeoning world of information possibilities. As will be explored, the results of such transformations for most ALA-accredited programs and for many library practitioners can now be viewed, in hindsight, as substantially negative.

The Worlds of Library Practice and Library Education in 1950

In studying the roots of the conflicting library and information intellectual traditions it is best to heed the warning of Robert K. Merton, the twentieth-century sociologist and intellectual giant, who noted that "the historian of ideas" is more likely to see intellectual ancestors where they do not exist than to overlook people important to an intellectual movement's theoretical development (1968, 8). In other words, constructing an extended history for the subordination of library to information before the 1950s, the period before the "official" establishment of information science, is more likely to be more misleading than helpful.

As has already been pointed out in the Chapter 3's "Noteworthy Events with Implications for North American Library and Information Education and Practice," the terms *information scientist* and *information science* did not gain wide acceptance until after the mid-1950s (Summers et al. 1999). Admittedly, within the author's historical summary can be found organizations whose members doubtlessly privileged "information" over "education" or "recreation" before there was an "information science," presumably including individual or organizational members of such groups as the Special Libraries Association (1909) and the American Documentation Institute (1937). Attempting to nail down information science's precise intellectual origins beyond the mid-twentieth century would be controversial, frustrating, and ultimately unproductive. Alternatively, both theory and common sense suggest that a defensible analysis of the results of the progressive dominance of information over library can begin around 1950, a year when "library" was being urged to more fully embrace an "information" orientation and when "information" as a field was on the verge of developing a self-definition.

Here it is necessary to return to a more in-depth consideration of the mid-twentieth-century *Public Library Inquiry* first addressed in Chapter 4. The reason for the additional review is quite simple; many of the contemporary problems facing libraries, particularly public libraries, are the long-term, negative legacy of libraries taking the "information turn" advocated by Robert D. Leigh and his research team. It is to be recalled that the *Inquiry* was charged with conducting the research deemed necessary to set the future direction for the post–World War II public library world. In Leigh's own words, "the problem set for the Inquiry was twofold: to appraise public libraries in terms of their own stated objectives and to appraise the appropriateness of the objectives themselves against the background of American social and cultural institutions and values" (Leigh 1950, 3–4). Taken as a whole, in the words of Douglas Raber, the *Public Library Inquiry* and its resulting publications represent a cumulative effort by Leigh and his collaborators "to provide librarianship with a theory, a diagnosis, and a strategy for action" (Raber 1994, 52). That the theory, diagnosis, and action strategy were later to be proved erroneous, does not detract from the reality that the research team and its leader did their best to help libraries and librarians thrive in the post–World War II world.

As part of this overall effort Leigh not only directed the *Public Library Inquiry* but also wrote *The Public Library in the United States* (1950). In this work he went beyond matters primarily germane to public libraries to devote a chapter to analyzing the ALA-accredited American and Canadian library education of his day (1950, 186–221). In a development that will resonate with the information combatants in the current information-library intellectual dispute, Leigh's Chapter 10, "Library Personnel and Training," contains his endorsement of the freedom to innovate in the curriculums of several library education programs that resulted from the mid-twentieth century's temporary cessation of accreditation by the practitioner-dominated ALA (1950, 221). Leigh, a political scientist and former president of Bennington College, describes the advantages of bringing to the instruction of students whose career interests involved library services to adults, the same sociological, psychological, and educational theories taught to their counterparts preparing for library work with children (216). Then and now, theory is important in justifying a discipline, field, or profession's place in the university world. It is particularly significant if the area involved cannot emulate business, law, or medicine in providing the parent academic institution with a larger tuition revenue stream and, ultimately, a critical number of prosperous or even wealthy alums who might be induced to contribute to annual or special fundraising campaigns and remember their alma mater in their wills.

Douglas Raber and Mary Niles Maack (1994) have discerned a number of long-term impacts of the *Public Library Inquiry* and its director, Robert D. Leigh, including a "sustained effort to create a new vision of the social role of the library" (46). However, they also stressed that the "impact" of "this broadened view" on the field of librarianship as a whole needs further exploration (46). This author believes that such a study might profitably address whether Leigh's theorizing about librarianship's connection with communication may have inspired his information science successors to achieve their contemporary dominance within ALA-accredited professional education.

Mid-Twentieth-Century Library Education

According to Leigh (1950), the thirty-four programs of library education then accredited by ALA were in the process of transitioning from the old model of a fifth year bachelor of library science (BLS) to supporting a one-year master's of library science (MLS) degree. His extensive research discerned that such programs had a distinct second-class status in the higher education environment and were far from being recognized as sources of campus intellectual leadership. Compared to other professional schools the ALA-accredited library programs were generally smaller in size and possessed fewer resources to support research. Leigh's explanation for such ills involved the claim that library educators could not rely on ALA to pressure their sponsoring universities or colleges to provide even a minimum level of university resources (191).

In general, the library education programs of 1950 offered a standard core or required curriculum. This usually consisted of four or five courses, dealing with "(1) cataloging and classification; (2) bibliography and reference; (3) book selection; (4) library administration; (5) history of libraries, books and printing" (Leigh 1950, 214). Since five required courses were clearly an insufficient professional preparation, curriculum "space" was available for additional study and the accredited programs of 1950 also taught elective and advanced courses in such specialties as children's services, cataloging, and reference. Additionally, classes addressing the needs of different types of libraries, including academic, school, special, and public, were provided on either the graduate or undergraduate level (Leigh 1950, 214).

As already noted, at the time of Leigh's writing (1950), the scope of the changes involved in transitioning from a BLS to an MLS professional degree had led ALA to withdraw "temporarily from the task of accreditation" (221). This withdrawal was seen by Leigh as a positive opportunity for "experimentation" (221). Then as now, ALA-accredited programs educated only a part of the ranks of new professionals entering the library job market every year. For example, non–ALA-accredited programs supported by teachers' colleges or university-based schools of education taught a large number of librarians, even if they were then (and now) supposedly receiving instruction in only the skills necessary to work in elementary, middle, and high school environments (Leigh 1950, 207).

Leigh asserted that the library was a primary means of communication but argued that it should abandon its emphasis on the general audience that was already satisfied by the mass media. Its true purpose was to meet the needs of only a select few—the "serious groups in the community" (234). Nonetheless, support yet existed in the mid-twentieth century for the dual concepts of the library as an educational institution and the librarian as educator (Lancour 1949/1971, 64). Leigh himself admitted that the "idea of a tax-supported institution such as the public library assuming the character of a general agency of out-of-school education is logically sound" but rejected the primacy of the library-education connection, largely on the basis of a perceived lack of interest and commitment by librarians to the concept and the historic lack of support from funding sources (1950, 226). Seemingly quixotically, without abandoning his view of the public library as part of the "whole field of communication," Leigh nevertheless endorsed the idea of schools of education cooperating with library schools to provide a "unified curriculum" for children's and school librarians (1950, 240). Even with his commitment to defining the public library by its information role and subordinating it within the intellectual realm of communication, the information science of his day, Leigh could not neglect the importance of the library's learning role.

In 1950, the faculty teaching in the ALA-accredited programs tended to lack doctoral degrees and had been hired more on their experience in libraries and effectiveness at teaching than any research ability. It was literally possible to retire from a position of a practitioner and, without any further education beyond the basic professional degree, be appointed to a faculty position within an ALA-accredited library education program. Taken as a whole, the result was a strong practitioner orientation and a relatively weak higher education affiliation that continued for several more decades. Nevertheless, there was a growing pressure for library schools to adopt university norms.

It cannot be sufficiently stressed that the library world of 1950 was not the information-dominated field that exists today. Each of the library's long-standing educational, informational, and recreational functions was still in competition to define the nature and future of the public library (Leigh 1950, 222–226). In retrospect, it is clear that Robert D. Leigh and the staff of the *Public Library Inquiry* brought an "agenda" to their work. For them, information provision was the dominant function of the public library. To this end, using what one might now term the "information lens," they interpreted the available evidence to summarize the functions of the public library as "to serve the community as a general center of reliable information and to provide opportunity and encouragement for people of all ages to educate themselves continuously" (223). Far from being the center of its community, the public library was to be seen as a minor component of the field of communication with its concentration on service to community elites to be justified on the basis of this understanding (Leigh 240; Raber and Maack 1994, 38).

One might not agree with the worth of Leigh's goal of positioning the library as a small yet significant player in the post–World War II communications world yet still acknowledge that this mid-twentieth-century vision almost perfectly parallels the contemporary subordination of librarianship under information science found in the introductory texts commonly used in ALA-accredited programs (Rubin 2004). Regardless, Leigh's argument that the field needed to achieve a more secure standing in the academic environment still has contemporary value. ALA-accredited programs are still unlikely to generate massive amounts of tuition, state assistance, and donations for their parent institutions. In consequence theory, the academic bread and butter of history, English, and similar fields not noted for attracting substantial outside revenue, acquires a greater importance. Leigh, both as a professor of political science and former college president, appreciated the value of a solid conceptual basis in justifying a place for librarianship within higher education. One can summarize much of his extended work by noting that he tried to offer the best guidance he could on the approach most likely to generate and use theory within librarianship in order to acquire a minimum level of academic respectability. Leigh made a point of stressing that library educators were beginning to use "sociological method and literature" (theory) in understanding the library's place in the community. More specifically, he pointed out that library education programs were applying psychological and educational findings "to interpret and adapt library materials to adults" in the "field of reader guidance and adult education," while noting that "these intellectual disciplines have previously been used mainly in relation to library work with children" (1950, 215–216).

In the 1950 world of American and Canadian higher education, with no information science or critical mass of information programs yet available, *communication was the premier information discipline*. The understanding that "alternate directions" (223) for creating the library's future were still available in the mid-twentieth-century library, in this case the public library, is necessary to appreciate the importance of Leigh's efforts to define the library as a communication entity. Associating librarianship with the field of communication in 1950 was an ambitious yet ultimately flawed approach to connecting library education with a then fashionable source of the relevant intellectual formulations being developed and applied by theorists to help American culture understand the post–World War II explosion in communication technologies.

While Leigh would accept the support of education as a valid secondary role for libraries, he found recreation, the third aspect of the public library's historic education-information-recreation triumvirate of services, to be entirely undeserving of public support. Translated into twenty-first-century terms, his equation of library with communication, coupled with his emphasis on the library's provision of information, defines the library as an agency of information dissemination, with the encouragement of education as only an acknowledged secondary role. Since Leigh lacked the knowledge provided by more recent research that recreational reading has a strong learning component (Ross, McKechnie, and Rothbauer 2006), it was understandable that he could depict the idea of the library being a free source of leisure reading as likely to condemn it permanently inferior status or "doom it to gradual extinction because of the greater resources, reach, and competitive skill of the commercial media of mass communication" (224).

Now: Librarianship in The Twenty-First Century

A Fifty-Plus-Year Overview

It is likely the case that the subsuming of library education under information instruction required (1) the creation of the new discipline of information science in the post-1950s academic world, and (2) the gradual intensification of pressure in higher education contexts for ALA-accredited programs to adopt university standards. It is noteworthy that the twentieth-century endeavor to adopt university benchmarks for appropriate faculty education and research actually predates Leigh's mid-century *Public Library Inquiry* by several decades. Unlike efforts to precisely outline the intellectual genealogy of information science, the effort to socialize library educators and, later, information science professors into higher education culture can be traced with some precision to the issuance of C. C. Williamson's 1923 *Training for Library Service: A Report Prepared for the Carnegie Corporation of New York* which argued for the connection of library schools with universities, instead of large city public libraries (Biggs 1985, 268).

Once library education became associated with higher education, particularly with research universities, there began what Mary Biggs (1985) saw as "a constant movement toward upgrading" the educational requirements and research and publication criteria required for library school faculty (272). In 1928 the University of Chicago had set the pattern not only for advanced education but also for subsuming "library" under other fields and disciplines by offering a Ph.D. taught by a faculty that "consisted of doctorate-holding scholars, committed to research and with weak or non-existent library backgrounds" (Biggs 1985, 270). Even though the first "library" doctoral program obviously could not recruit Ph.D. holders in librarianship for its faculty, the deliberate absence of scholars with extensive library backgrounds sent out a strong signal that practitioner relevance was not a priority in the most research intensive ALA-accredited program.

Other ALA-accredited programs would later offer a Ph.D. in library science but the tradition of relying on faculty with doctorates from other areas without a substantial past association with libraries always threatened to make librarianship, later information science, subject to "colonization" by academics unable to achieve their career aspirations in the disciplines where they received their advanced degree. A reasonable comparison with another professional field would be the absurdity of operating a school of social work through employing physicists, historians, or psychologists without any experience in the actual practice of social work. Apparently, all things are possible, often to the detriment of practitioners, if one defines a field as multidisciplinary. In this context, in 2005, Terry L. Weech and Marian Pluzhenskaia would confidently predict that "by 2006 the majority of faculty in schools of LIS will have doctorates outside the LIS discipline," a development that "would seem to confirm the multidisciplinarity of LIS education in the United States and Canada" (2005, 157).

Since ALA, through its accreditation process, performs a semi-governmental function, the author has been comfortable defining the process through which nonlibrarians redefine and dominate what used to be the programs of library education as a clear example of "regulatory capture" (Ehrenhalt 2004; Faure-Grimaud and Martimort 2003). As discussed in Chapter 4, this particular capture, at first involving individual programs and later encompassing the entire ALA accreditation system also represents a near textbook example of the theorizing of Scott Frickel and Neil Gross in "A General Theory of Scientific/ Intellectual Movements" (2005).

The Resistance to Practitioners Reclaiming Control Over the Accreditation Process

The Association for Library and Information Science Education (ALISE) has been dominated in recent years by information advocates, albeit with occasional resistance by "library" educators to the ever-present "information discourse." In consequence, the annual conferences of this association, in years past devoted to matters of library education, now offer frequent examples of the pernicious effects of information's regulatory capture on the ALA process of accreditation, including a strong resistance by information faculty to demands by library practitioners for a relevant *library* education. In 2005 the ALISE annual conference produced a particularly significant attack on the very concept of a required "core curriculum" as part of John Leslie King's virtuoso presentation "Stepping Up: Shaping the Future of the Field" (2005). At the time King was serving as the dean of the University of Michigan's School of Information. Not content with making some strong, if debatable, arguments in favor of the subordination of librarianship to information, King made what might best be described as a blatant threat to bring down the ALA system of accreditation if practitioners continue to forget their place and persist in their demands that professors in ALA-accredited programs provide a practitioner version of an appropriate library education. Before addressing the real issues and rhetorical lapses in that part of King's attack on the very idea of required core courses, it is useful to consider what exactly might be demanded if the ALA succeeded in its effort to secure instructional relevance.

As of this writing (July 2007), yet another body of ALA, in this case a Presidential Task Force on Library Education appointed by 2006–2007 ALA President Leslie Burger, is working diligently to "help describe the new normal for library education" with a report expected by the association's 2008 Annual Conference in Anaheim, California (Burger 2007, 5). The author obviously lacks the prescience to discuss the details of a 2008 report in 2007. However, in 2004, prior to his own 2005–2006 term as ALA president, Michael Gorman, the noted critic of information-dominated library education, outlined the following elements for a contemporary core curriculum in programs accredited by ALA—"collection development and acquisitions; cataloging; reference and library instruction; circulation, maintenance, preservation, etc.; systems; management; types of library" (Gorman 2004, 378).

If readers will examine Robert D. Leigh's findings concerning the professional education offered in 1950 (above), they will discern, with the exception of "systems," that the core areas of the mid-twentieth-century curriculum align remarkably well with the twenty-first-century requirements advocated by Gorman. Obviously the matters to be addressed in the twenty-first century would reflect more than fifty years of progress in technology and, one hopes, a similar growth in the understandings achieved through the social sciences whose assistance in library matters was so applauded by Leigh. In their details, two sections of a similarly named course offered a half-century apart would be expected to exhibit considerable differences. Gorman does not seem to be frozen in time and opposed to any alterations in the content of core courses so long as their evolution is in response to changing library realities. His particular concern seems to be that the upgraded versions of the 1950 core courses no longer seem to be required as a basic professional education in a number of ALA-accredited programs (2004).

Unlike Gorman, John Leslie King (2005) sees it as a positive that ALA-accredited programs have been abandoning a set of required courses as such programs evolve and independently develop their own curriculums. In this context, he made it clear that he was the dean of an information school, not a library school (16). His response to Gorman and other critics who believe that the present system of ALA accreditation abandons library in favor of information because the process is controlled by the very programs it seeks to accredit, may be paraphrased as follows:

1. There is no problem with the present, nonstandardized curriculum in ALA-accredited programs.
2. Furthermore, elite institutions do not need ALA accreditation. Such institutions are to be accorded appropriate deference and their decisions on what courses to offer—or not offer—are no concern at all of library practitioners and their elected officers.
3. Given the present circumstances, efforts by ALA to enforce a "core curriculum" will fail. Any accreditation process only works because elite educational institutions agree to participate and give the process credibility. This participation of elite institutions even makes possible the accreditation of "less elite educational institutions."
4. There are two basic reasons why efforts by the ALA to mandate a core curriculum will fail. Such efforts will be rejected as

being unjust or they will drive elite institutions out of the system, a withdrawal that will bring about the destruction of the ALA accreditation structure.

5. The ability of university faculty to experiment with the curriculum is of great value to the future of all the components of the information professions, including the small component known as librarianship. This freedom of faculty to innovate is much more important than the issue of whether or not current practitioners view the curriculum as relevant to their professional needs (2005, 15).

In addition to telling ALA and its members to be satisfied with the education offered by their accredited programs, King expressed his irritation at complaints from practitioners that programs such as his had dropped "library" from their names. While he allows that the change might have meant something to those affected at the actual time "library" was deleted from the program title, he saw any later complaints about the transformation as irrelevant. On the more positive side he did suggest that if ALA follows his advice and allows the elite programs to deliver a professional education as each program sees fit, such leading programs will obviously have no reason to given up their accreditation and thereby destroy the accreditation system (2005, 16).

Evaluating King's Threats

On the whole, John Leslie King's 2005 ALISE presentation may best be considered as an unusually well-constructed example of the relentless demand of many (but not all) faculty in ALA-accredited programs that library practitioners stop their complaining and accept the faculty's "trust us, we know what we are doing" approach to the professional education curriculum. To these professors advisory committees are fine, particularly since past experience suggests that their recommendations can either be ignored or modified to suit faculty interests. Mandating course content is quite another thing and, for King, must be resisted. Since persuasion did not seem to be working and practitioners were still bothering his and the other research university faculty with their demands for a relevant education, King proved perfectly willing to escalate the argument to the level of threats. For him, it was clear that the faculty's "right" to "define the question" and to provide the appropriate answers through information science research and coursework was being undermined and such undermining was not to be tolerated. Intellectual formulations regarding meaning and purpose are the prerogative of the faculty, not the practitioner.

To borrow from Jean Bethke Elshtain's fine appraisal of the pragmatist theorist and Nobel Prize-winner Jane Addams, King's remarks, like so many assertions of other "information absolutists," exemplify the "unpardonable sin of intellect [which] is to create an overarching ideological system that tries to force life to conform to its model" (2001, 86). In the case of the library world, practitioners seem to exhibit an unreasonable tendency to disregard information science theory, particularly its fundamental premise that libraries are all about information, and King finds such questioning to be intolerable.

At bottom, King and other information advocates see practitioner questioning of course and degree relevance as immaterial to an "elite" university program. Librarians should be thankful that professors associated with "elite" institutions even agree to participate at all in any system of accreditation operated by a library association.

Given the history of higher education in the state of Michigan, the demand of a former University of Michigan dean that library practitioners cease agitating for an education appropriate what they perceive to be to the realities of their working lives is only to be expected. Readers may not know that the University of Michigan holds a unique place within public higher education. The author once had the opportunity to talk with a president emeritus of a public research university regarding which institution he and his former associates within the National Association of State Universities and Land-Grant Colleges (NASULGC) saw as a model to be emulated. Expecting to be told the University of California, Berkeley, or the University of California, Los Angeles, the author was surprised to learn that the University of Michigan was held by experienced presidents to be the public institution most worthy of emulation. The reason was simple, in its wisdom—or in its folly—the state of Michigan has made its flagship university virtually independent of all outside influence. Simply stated, professors and administrators at the University of Michigan are so protected from the consequences of their actions outside the campus environment that they have become accustomed to telling the residents and politicians of their state to "go away and mind your own business" with no fear of reprisal. That Dean (now Vice Provost) King would feel entitled to instruct an ALA president and tens of thousands of his library supporters to do the precisely the same thing simply reflects the history of privilege so long associated with his university.

As will be discussed in Chapter 6, such resistance to offering a practitioner mandated library education may be a tactic that can produce unexpectedly negative outcomes for professors in state universities with ALA-accredited programs. Even the privileged University of Michigan may find it advisable to respond to the demands for relevancy by the library profession if the case can be made in the larger public arena that the refusal of the university to provide an appropriate professional education hampers the ability of Michigan librarians to help solve critical state and local problems. The capacity to demonstrate the library profession's responsiveness to the needs of its service communities is absolutely crucial to creating positive futures for both libraries and librarians in academic, public, and school environments. The first step necessary in this process is to identify and build upon the reasons why people, including community leaders and politicians, value their libraries and their librarians.

References

Abbott, Andrew. 1988. *The System of Professions: An Essay on the Division of Expert Labor.* Chicago: University of Chicago Press.

Barzun, Jacques. 1978. The professions under siege. *Harper's* (October): 61–66, 68.

Bates, Marcia J. 2004. Information science at the University of California at Berkeley in the 1960s: A memoir of student days. *Library Trends* 52, no. 4 (spring): 683–701.

Biggs, Mary. 1985. Who/what/why should a library educator be? *Journal of Education for Library and Information Science* 25, no. 4 (spring): 262–278.

Burger, Leslie. 2007. Changing library education. Instructional program transformation is key to the profession. *American Libraries* 38, no. 4 (April): 5.

Cronin, Blaise. 2002. Holding the center while prospecting at the periphery: Domain identity and coherence in North American information studies education. *Education for Information* 20, no. 1 (March): 3–10.

Crowley, Bill. 1998. Dumping the "Library." *Library Journal* 120 (July): 48–49.

———. 1999. The control and direction of professional education. *Journal of the American Society for Information Science,* 50, no. 12 (October): 1127–1135.

———. 2005. *Spanning the Theory-Practice Divide in Library and Information Science.* Lanham, MD: Scarecrow Press.

Crowley, Bill, and Deborah Ginsberg. 2003. Intracultural reciprocity, information ethics, and the survival of librarianship in the 21st century. *In Ethics and*

Electronic Information: A Festschrift for Stephen Almagno, ed. Tom Medina and Barbara Rockenbach, 94–107. Jefferson, NC: McFarland, 2003.

———. 2005. Professional values: Priceless. *American Libraries* 36, no. 1 (January): 52–55.

Cuban, Larry. 1999. *How Scholars Trumped Teachers: Change Without Reform in University Curriculum, Teaching, and Research, 1890–1990.* New York: Teachers College Press.

Ehrenhalt, Alan. 2004. Assessments: Spreading out the clout. *Governing* (April): 6, 8.

Elshtain, Jean Bethke. 2001. Jane Addams and the social claim. *Public Interest* 145 (fall): 82–92.

Faure-Grimaud, Antoine, and David Martimort. 2003. Regulatory inertia. *RAND Journal of Economics* 34, no. 3 (autumn): 413–437.

Fialkoff, Francine. 2007. Lusting after Ohio's libraries. *Library Journal* 132, no. 10 (1 June): 8.

Frickel, Scott, and Neil Gross. 2005. A general theory of scientific/intellectual movements. *American Sociological Review* 70, no. 2 (April): 204–232.

Gorman, Michael. 2004. Whither library education? *New Library World* 105, nos. 1204/1205 (September): 376–380.

Haycock, Ken. 2000. The congress on professional education in North America. Paper presented at the 66th IFLA Council and General Conference, Jerusalem, Israel. http://www.ifla.org/IV/ifla66/papers/146-156e.htm (accessed March 29, 2007).

Hildreth, Charles R., and Michael Koenig. 2002. Organizational realignment of LIS programs in academia: From independent standalone units to incorporated programs. *Journal of Education for Library and Information Science* 43, no. 2 (spring): 126–133.

KALIPER (Project). *Educating Library and Information Science Professionals for a New Century, the KALIPER Report.* 2000. Reston, VA: KALIPER Advisory Committee, Association for Library and Information Science Education (ALISE).

King, John Leslie. 2005. Stepping Up: Shaping the Future of the Field. Plenary Session 3 presentation, Friday, January 14, at the ALISE 2005 Conference. dLIST http://dlist.sir.arizona.edu/739 (accessed June 27, 2007).

Koenig, Michael E. D., and Charles Hildreth. 2002. The end of the standalone "library school." *Library Journal* 127, no. 11 (June 15): 40–41.

Kuhn, Thomas S. 1970. *The Structure of Scientific Revolutions,* 2nd ed. Chicago: University of Chicago Press.

Lancour, Harold. (1949/1971). Discussion. In *Education for Librarianship: Papers Presented at the Library Conference, University of Chicago, August 16–21, 1948,* ed. Bernard Berelson, 59–65. Rpt. Freeport, NY: Books for Libraries Press.

Leigh, Robert D. 1950. *The Public Library in the United States.* New York: Columbia University Press, 1950.

Maines, David R., Jeffrey C. Bridger, and Jeffery T. Ulmer. 1996. Mythic facts and Park's pragmatism: On predecessor-selection and theorizing in human ecology. *Sociological Quarterly* 37 (3): 521–549.

Mead, George Herbert. [1932] 1959. *The Philosophy of the Present.* LaSalle, IL: Open Court.

Merton, Robert King. 1968. *Social Theory and Social Structure.* New York: Free Press.

Neustadt, Richard E., and Ernest R. May. 1986. *Thinking in Time: The Uses of History for Decision Makers.* New York: Free Press.

Perceptions of Libraries and Information Resources: A Report to the OCLC Membership. 2005. Principal contributors, Cathy De Rosa et al. Dublin, OH: OCLC Online Computer Library Center. http://www.oclc.org/reports/2005perceptions.htm (accessed September 22, 2006).

Raber, Douglas. 1994. Inquiry as ideology: The politics of the public library inquiry. *Libraries and Culture* 29, no. 1 (winter): 49–60.

Raber, Douglas, and Mary Niles Maack. 1994. Scope background, and intellectual context of the Public Library Inquiry. *Libraries and Culture* 29, no. 1 (winter): 26–48.

Ross, Catherine Sheldrick, Lynne (E.F.) McKechnie, and Paulette M. Rothbauer. 2006. *Reading Matters: What the Research Reveals about Reading, Libraries, and Community.* Westport, CT: Libraries Unlimited.

Rubin, Richard E. 2004. *Foundations of Library and Information Science,* 2nd ed. New York: Neal-Schuman.

Summers, Ron, Charles Oppenheim, Jack Meadows, Cliff McKnight, and Margaret Kinnell. 1999. Information science in 2010. A Loughborough University view. *Journal of the American Society for Information Science* 50, no. 12 (October): 1153–1162.

Upon the Objects to be Attained by the Establishment of a Public Library: Report of The Trustees of The Public Library of the City of Boston, July 1852. Boston Public Library: 1852. City Document—No. 27 J.H. Eastburn, City Printer, http://www.scls.lib.wi.us/mcm/history/report_of_trustees.html (accessed December 11, 2006).

Weech, Terry L., and Marina Pluzhenskaia. 2005. LIS education and multidisciplinarity: An exploratory study. *Journal of Education for Library and Information Science* 46, no. 2 (spring): 154–164.

Wilson, Patrick. 1983. *Second-Hand Knowledge: An Inquiry into Cognitive Authority.* Westport, CT: Greenwood Press.

Wingett, Yvonne. 2007. Gilbert library to be first to drop Dewey decimal. *Arizona Republic.* May 30. http://www.azcentral.com/news/articles/0530nodewey0530.html (accessed May 31, 2007).

CHAPTER 6

Restoring the Balance

THE LICENSURE "SOLUTION"

Slightly more than a year ago, students in the author's section of the introductory course at Dominican University's Graduate School of Library and Information Science were in the midst of a heated exchange over whether programs offering American Library Association–accredited master's degrees were properly educating aspiring librarians, information specialists, and knowledge managers. Although this was the first graduate course for many of the students, quite a few were already working in libraries or corporate information centers, often full-time. They and other students were communicating regularly with friends who had earlier earned their degrees from various ALA-accredited programs, including Dominican University, and were subscribing to such electronic forums as Publib, mentioned in the previous chapter; NEWLIB-L, the "discussion list for librarians new to the profession who wish to share experiences and discuss ideas"; and a number of other specialized online discussion lists.

These electronic and in-person sources of career information, as well as the more formal library media, provided the students with quite a few disconcerting stories. In the public and academic library areas such tales included accounts of the deprofessionalization of librarian positions, often conveyed through postings or off-list communications from list members who were describing the situation at their library. Such accounts sometimes reported that library managers, for cost-saving purposes or the search for a higher status in national rankings, were reconfiguring librarian positions downward to the associate, assistant, or even clerical level. Alternatively, it was often the case that employers were dividing full-time librarian positions into part-time jobs in order to avoid paying benefits.

In addition to the accounts of negative job transformations, some librarians sharing career information with the students were more than a bit annoyed at what they saw as another lapse by the programs awarding them their ALA-accredited master's degrees. It seems that as students they had not been informed about a new and lower level on the academic and public librarian career ladders, particularly in desirable metropolitan areas. More so than in the past, it appears to be the case that inexperienced academic and public librarians who are not geographically flexible may have to work two part-time librarian positions in the hope that one will eventually evolve into a full-time job. Alternatively, if already employed, new graduates tied to a given community may continue longer in their positions as librarian assistants or clerks even as their student loan payments loom large in the near future. New holders of the ALA-accredited master's degree without significant local ties seem to have a much easier time securing full-time professional positions.

As is often the case, one of the students in the introductory course was an attorney with a Chicago law firm who was in the process of making a career switch to law librarianship. Just as the discussion was trailing off, this student pointed out, "The problem is a lack of licensure. In Illinois only school librarians are licensed and have to take specific courses that prepare them for the state test. If other librarians were like attorneys and had to pass the equivalent of the bar in order to practice, students might have an easier time finding employment."

THE ELUSIVE DREAM OF PROFESSIONAL LICENSURE

On the surface, professional licensure for librarians has the appeal of being simple and plausible. Licensure is usually justified on the basis that it encourages the development of greater expertise through an incentive for people to invest their time and money in acquiring superior knowledge and skill in order to practice a profession at a higher level, presumably to the public benefit. It is often opposed on the theory that licensure, by requiring a more costly preparation, limits the number of competitors for jobs and increases the cost of the services provided (Parker, Bower, and Weissman 2002). In consequence, state or provincial legislators, who in theory are elected to govern for the benefit of the public, need to be convinced that licensing a profession (a) helps solve a crucial public problem, and (b) does so in a manner where the public benefit is worth the additional cost. Admittedly, these criteria can be waived if a profession has sufficient political influence to secure the necessary laws and regulations, regardless of the strength of its argument.

In nations where barbers, hairstylists, and cosmetologists have joined attorneys and physicians in securing state or provincial licensure, the question naturally arises why many librarians have not done the same. It would be a mistake to embrace the simplest explanation that the services of a library or information center are more valued than the professional expertise of those who provide them. The reality is a bit more complicated and often varies by context.

Public Libraries

A 2003 review of public library "standards and guidelines" from all fifty American states found that only twenty-four had "mandatory certification or educational training requirements" for public librarians, with considerable difference in the levels of education needed. Degree and experience levels varied greatly with some states requiring certification for only the head county librarian (Arizona, Texas) while others, for example New Jersey, stipulating that librarians have a master's degree from "an approved library program" (Hamilton-Pennell 2003, 10).

For the most part, setting and enforcing a requirement of a master's degree from an ALA-accredited program for a public librarian position has not been enacted into law or required under a state or provincial regulation; it tends to remain the prerogative of county or municipal civil service systems or a library's board of trustees. Should these bodies downgrade any or most of their librarian positions to reduce personnel costs by requiring less education, there is little to be done to resist such deprofessionalization except where a union contract may be in play.

At the risk of being accused of blaming the victim, it is useful to remind the reader of a management truism, often attributed to Herb White, the former dean of the School of Library and Information Science, Indiana University, Bloomington, that "in the absence of money there is always money." In both the United States and Canada money is a significant indicator of value, and scarce public resources tend to flow to sectors that have proven their worth to communities and their leaders. It is too often the case that the public library's "lack of marketing, impassive advocacy and isolation from the community" (Public Agenda Foundation 2006, 13) have prevented it from making the case for the dollars needed to help solve community problems to the satisfaction of local political leaders and the general public.

Academic Libraries

The Board of Directors of the Association of College and Research Libraries (ACRL), the relevant division of ALA, voted in 2001 to reaffirm its 1975 policy statement that "the master's degree in library science from a library school program accredited by the American Library Association is the appropriate terminal professional degree for academic librarians" (ACRL 2001). However, this sector has also experienced a relentless deprofessionalization or downgrading of previously "librarian" positions (Crowley and Ginsberg 2005, 52) coupled, almost quixotically, with a substitution of a Ph.D. in another discipline and a period of apprenticeship in an academic library for the ALA-accredited master's degree (Crowley 2004).

School Libraries

In most states, only school librarians or school library media specialists are required to have licensure *in their educational/instructional role as teachers.* The effect on employment opportunities for new graduates of such state certification can be extremely positive, as in northeast Illinois, or can be particularly limited, as in the Appalachian counties of southeast Ohio. A number of American states and Canadian provinces do not mandate the employment of school librarians while others have gone as far as to remove existing regulations that require they be a part of the educational program offered at either the building or the school system level (Crowley and Ginsberg 2003, 102).

In Canada, it is a challenging fact of political life for teacher librarians (school librarians) that "funding for school libraries is included in the block funding that [British Columbia's] Government allocates to school districts" and that the BC authorities leave the allocation of such dollars to locally elected school boards (van Dyk personal communication, 2007). If the British Columbia Teacher-Librarians' Association's regularly issued annual surveys of working and learning conditions (2006) and the Ontario Library Association's *School Libraries & Student Achievement in Ontario* (2006) are to be believed, Canada's ignorance of the value of teacher-librarians almost rivals that of the "great republic to the south." It is indicative of a real lack of appreciation that "only 18% of school libraries have a full-time teacher librarian" in British Columbia (British Columbia Teacher-Librarians' Association

2006, 5), despite the reality that research elsewhere in Canada joins prior American analyses in demonstrating that the work of teacher librarians directly contributes to student proficiency in—and enjoyment of—reading (Ontario Library Association 2006, 2). Unfortunately, the progress promised by such studies can be thwarted by the reality that, in Canada, "through neglect, too many school libraries are now little more than storage rooms" (Haycock 2003, 9).

Special Libraries and Information/Knowledge Centers

However termed, the educational requirements for professional librarians and information/knowledge specialists in tax-supported, specialized government units are usually determined by state, provincial, or local civil service rules. For-profit entities in the private sector—a primary employment area for true information specialists—are usually exempt from government-required qualifications and have the freedom to hire according to institutional or corporate policies.

Consequences of the Failure to Achieve Licensure

In much of English-speaking North America, a master's degree from an ALA-accredited program does not lead to licensure and the enhanced employment prospects that would otherwise accrue to those who have earned this credential. This state of affairs has both demonstrable and symbolic impacts, usually negative, regarding employment prospects and career longevity. The responsibility is shared by practitioners, educators, and the ALA bureaucracy, components of the system of professional preparation which have pursued their own ends to the detriment of the common good. It represents a type of human dilemma that was eloquently described in Garrett Hardin's "The Tragedy of the Commons" (1968).

Briefly summarized, Hardin's often cited article uses the example of the medieval village commons where residents long pastured their cattle. He described the natural human tendency of the villagers to keep increasing the size of their own herds to maximize their individual gain. Unfortunately, every villager acting to her or his private advantage in the use of this shared resource hastened its decline through often unchecked overgrazing. A system with the continuing potential to benefit all involved simply broke down (1968, 162). For purposes of discussion one can substitute "professional librarianship" for Hardin's common grazing land. Based on the analyses provided in the earlier chapters of this volume the reader ought not to be surprised to learn that the author believes that the pursuit of self-interest by practitioners, educators, and ALA alike, has brought the ALA system of accreditation to the brink of self-destruction.

It is to be recalled that the author titled this work *Renewing Professional Librarianship: A Fundamental Rethinking* and explained in Chapter 1 that its basic purpose is to explore how professional librarianship can be safeguarded and enhanced in the new millennium. In consequence, the reader might justifiably expect that the author, in this final chapter, will both recapitulate the negative effects of practitioners, educators, and ALA bureaucrats pursing their own interests and offer a number of suggestions for their alleviation.

What Do The Various "Publics" Want From Their Libraries?

At some point even the most uncompromising information theorists must accept that school and academic libraries tend to be physically located within, or are supported online by, educational institutions. While university and school libraries can and do assist professors and teachers in conducting research, the fact remains that the education of students is the primary justification for the local taxes, state assistance, or tuition revenue that flows to the parent institution. It would be necessary to subtract the students and turn a university or school into a research institute for its library or media center to function under the information paradigm instead of the educational/ learning model.

In the end, with corporate and research information specialists claimed by the information science field and academic and school libraries solidly in the educational-learning field we term librarianship, the contested area for theoretical jurisdiction has often been the public library. While information theorists would argue otherwise, the evidence of repeated surveys such as the recently published *Long Overdue: A Fresh Look at Public and Leadership Attitudes About Libraries in the 21st Century* (Public Agenda Foundation 2006) reveals that the public and community leadership embrace the learning model of the public library. Years ago, Patrick Williams, a Dominican University professor, fittingly summarized this reality by concluding *The American Public Library and the Problem of Purpose* with the words, "the American public has always wanted and still wants the public library to be an educational institution. And, in all probability, the public will not have it otherwise" (1988, 137). The words of Williams can and do resonate equally well in Canadian contexts (Burnaby Public Library [2006]; Crowley 2007).

Legislation and Government Policy

For more than a century, state governments have made it clear through a history of legislation allowing tax support for public libraries that such institutions were and are educational and learning institutions (Crowley 2006, 78). Since public libraries are long-established entities, the concerns that now reach the level of state, provincial, and national legislatures tend to deal more with adequacy of library funding than with the public library's fundamental purpose. However, a discussion of a nation's justification for supporting the library was precisely what emerged during 2004 and 2005 in Great Britain when the Culture, Media and Sport Committee of the House of Commons carried out extensive hearings in a wide-ranging exploration of public library matters, addressing areas from accessibility, funding, and service provision and policy to the recruitment of library staff and issues regarding the provision of information through the electronic People's Network (Great Britain 2005a, 5).

The resulting House of Commons report is a two-volume work titled *Public Libraries*. In the first paragraph of the summary of its findings, the Culture, Media and Sport Committee, having forced itself to choose between the concepts of the public library as a *learning institution* or the public library as a *provider of information*, came down foursquare on the side of learning, with a particular emphasis on promoting reading. The importance of the rationale for this choice suggests the need to quote the paragraph in full.

> Public libraries are an important national resource with a vital role to play in establishing, nurturing and nourishing people's love of reading. Libraries also play an important part in life-long and informal learning providing access to books as well as other reading material whether on paper or, via the People's Network, in digital form.

Libraries, together with their staff, are a trusted civic amenity—highly valued, safe public spaces and storehouses of advice, information and knowledge—without which the citizens of Britain would be very much the poorer. (Great Britain 2005a, 3)

A careful reading of the massive amount of oral and written testimony collected in volume 2 of *Public Libraries* (2005b) reveals that this House of Commons committee insured that it was made fully aware of the many roles of the public library, including providing access to information technology, the Internet, and "a range of other services not traditionally seen as part of a library's core remit [responsibility]" (Great Britain 2005a, 16). Nonetheless, while the committee found such services to be important it held that the reading and other educational functions of the public library ranked higher in terms of public value and policy. To paraphrase Patrick Williams, (above) the public library is primarily an educational/learning entity and *the public and the legislature will not have it otherwise.*

Assigning Responsibility and Devising Solutions

Unintended Consequences

Looking back beyond the slow decades during which information established its dominance within ALA-accredited programs, it is possible to perceive a particularly arresting irony—the library community of 1950, with its awareness of librarianship's triad of responsibilities, education, information, recreation, was conceptually better situated to make its case for support to its various publics. The potentially fatal consequences for professional librarianship flowing from the fact that information science did not formally break off into a separate field but subsumed librarianship within the ALA system of education include the:

1. difficulty of justifying the library to its funding sources due to the inapplicability of information theory to solving critical problems in the majority of library concerns and contexts;
2. failure of information science to fulfill its claim to secure a leadership role for its degree holders in the globalized information economy.

Briefly elaborated, aside from business and research contexts, the many publics served by the "library" have not accepted the view that the primary role of libraries and librarians is information provision. While the information science concepts offered in ALA-accredited programs have well served corporate information and knowledge managers, they have mal-educated several generations of professionals for academic, public, and school libraries. The harm is compounded by the fact that information science did not deliver on its early promises to provide librarians with qualitative advantages in the competition with the contemporary "informatics" graduates of business, medicine, law, and the other programs that are now—or will shortly be—emerging in response to the lure of electronic information's multibillion-dollar markets. It is increasingly the case that the skills for professional success in managing information resources in a globalized marketplace can be taught in virtually any field or discipline with access to appropriate databases and professors able to convey effective analysis and communications strategies.

In order to overcome the unintended but nevertheless negative consequences flowing from exalting information within ALA-accredited programs and minimizing the education, learning, and reading roles of librarianship, it will be necessary for all the sectors whose actions have contributed to creating the problem to take strong action to remediate it. In this context, drawing on the previous chapters, it is worthwhile to again address the questions raised by former ALA President Michael Gorman and first discussed in Chapter 4.

As will be recalled, Gorman concluded his *New Library World* article with the following questions.

- Can library education and information science coexist in harmony without detriment to either or must they divorce?
- Can the ALA and the LIS schools work together to produce a national core curriculum?
- Can we revamp the accreditation system so that it is based on nationally agreed standards?
- Can we reconceptualize librarianship to make it attractive to future generations of librarians (Gorman 2004, 380)?

The author would like to believe that the present work, *Renewing Professional Librarianship: A Fundamental Rethinking*, represents a contribution to the effort to reconceptualize librarianship. Although the authors might protest, it is likely that contributions such as John E. Buschman's engagement with the marketplace mentality in his *Dismantling the Public Sphere: Situating and Sustaining Librarianship in the Age of the New Public Philosophy* (2003); Ronald B. McCabe's argument for renewal of the public library's community instructional mission in his *Civic Librarianship: Renewing the Social Mission of the Public Library* (2001); and Wayne Wiegand's encouragement of librarians to view their services from a cultural perspective and from the standpoint of the user (2001, 2003, 2005), inevitably lead back to a larger consideration of the library's commitment to support reading and lifelong learning.

It will be up to the reader to determine the extent of such contributions to the task of re-envisioning librarianship. Gorman's other questions, dealing with the coexistence of librarianship and information science, a common core curriculum, and national standards will be addressed below. By now the reader should understand that the evidence has convinced the author that there is no future for professional librarians in being defined as minor human components of the information infrastructure in a world of information self-service. Even so, he continues to acknowledge that the same information model accurately represents the increasingly competitive work environment of corporate and research information professionals. Librarianship with its primary commitment to learning and information science with its base in information analysis, are simply distinct fields for which aspiring professionals need different educational preparation. How such differences may be addressed by the overlapping yet nevertheless distinct subcultures involved with the system of ALA-accreditation— ALA itself, information and library educators, and practitioner communities—will now be considered.

The American Library Association: Reversing The Captured Culture of Accreditation

There are two strong indicators of the regulatory capture of the ALA accreditation system by the programs ALA so certifies. First, the schools of library and information studies now redefining themselves as information schools have long possessed the right to set their own degree requirements and continue to resist any efforts to restrict their ability to do so (Cronin 2000; King 2005). Second, it is a well-known fact that the "revolving door phenomenon" (Dal Bo 2006, 218) characteristic of regulatory capture is in play. A number of recent directors of the ALA Office for Accreditation assumed their position after having previously taught and researched in an ALA-accredited program. Furthermore, after serving at ALA, they went on to head several of the very same educational programs that the office was set up to help accredit. This statement of fact does not imply that the individuals involved were in any way exhibiting less than the highest professional standards. It simply suggests that the change in employment from heading the Office for Accreditation to directing an ALA-accredited program may well have been facilitated by shared beliefs, including a support for programs setting their own standards and a prioritization of the information model in the definition of the field of library and information studies.

SUGGESTIONS FOR REFORM AT THE ALA ACCREDITATION LEVEL

Change the Definition of the Field

Before any other reforms are undertaken, ALA needs to change the current definition of library and information studies to specifically include a commitment to lifelong learning and reading. As previously explored, the overwhelmingly information-oriented nature of the present description of the field is particularly evident if one deletes the only two mentions of "library" in its official description.

> The phrase "library and information studies" is understood to be concerned with recordable information and knowledge and the services and technologies to facilitate their management and use. Library and information studies encompasses information and knowledge creation, communication, identification, selection, acquisition, organization and description, storage and retrieval, preservation, analysis, interpretation, evaluation, synthesis, dissemination, and management. (ALA 1992, 2)

This definition of the field is particularly useful for ALA-accredited programs which use it to justify hiring as library and information studies professors Ph.D. holders from almost any field or discipline taught in the modern university. However, when used as a guide for developing and teaching the courses necessary to educate future academic, public, and school librarians, the result is to foster increasing irrelevance. The definition does describe much of the work of original catalogers. However, it is often inapplicable for the public-oriented learning and educational efforts of librarians and library staff that are so well demonstrated through effective children's storytelling, encouraging primary school students to read through selecting books fit for their purposes, teaching new college students the "tricks of the online searching trade," whether it be databases or search engines, and working with university faculty to better use knowledge tools to design new classes or develop theories relevant to practitioner needs.

As currently written, it is impossible to twist this definition of library and information studies so that circulating books, telling stories, organizing public programs, and operating a library art gallery can be covered by what is a barely disguised restatement of hard-core information science. On several occasions, the author has offered another definition of library science or librarianship that the reader might review to determine whether it or the ALA definition of the library and information studies field better fits what her or his academic, public, or school library actually does.

> As a field, library science or librarianship is concerned with understanding and advancing learning throughout the human lifecycle, with a particular emphasis on the processes of reading and other forms of communicating story, information, and meaning through library and library-related contexts. The emphasis on human learning, content, and meaning distinguishes library science from the newer field of information science. (Crowley 2007, 7)

The author does not presume to suggest substituting this definition of librarianship for the current ALA description of library and information studies. Rather, he suggests that it be mined—along with other sources—as a starting place for amending the current, information-centric definition to include reference to the library's roles in support of education, learning, and reading, in addition to its already acknowledged information commitment.

Implement Required Cores and Dual Majors

During the writing of this book the author, after again reading John Leslie King's denigration of the ALA system of accreditation (2005), seriously considered proposing a negative answer to the first part of Gorman's question, "Can library education and information science co-exist in harmony without detriment to either or must they divorce?" (Gorman 2004, 380). A strong argument can be made that information science and librarianship have evolved into different fields with a focus on solving different societal problems. However, the author is also a pragmatist. The unwillingness to engage with practitioners on their own terms is far from pandemic among all information educators. In addition, any effort to cleanse the library educational "house" of information education will be strongly resisted by both the information and the library faculty. Trying to separate the library sheep from the information goats (or vice versa) is guaranteed to result in the breakdown of the current system of accreditation.

And what is there to gain for ALA in dismantling the present accreditation process? In the wake of such an action, the nation's largest library association will lose its influence over the preparation of librarians and the vacuum left is likely to be filled by individual state and provincial forms of certification, with or without the requirement for a master's degree. In such an environment, education departments and schools may well expand their current school library media offerings and entrepreneurial community colleges are likely to present their existing library assistant courses as inexpensive substitutes. Master's degrees in school librarianship/school library media from university colleges of education might well be accepted as adequate preparation for public or academic librarians by state or provincial library regulators, campuses, and communities. Alternatively, if a community-college based education for the field of librarianship develops, the field will be effectively deprofessionalized.

The impact of the absence of ALA accreditation on academic librarianship, a sector of the field already possessing a second-class status within many colleges and universities because its master's degree requirement falls short in cultures where the Ph.D. is the accepted faculty standard, might best be described as an extended catastrophe. Public libraries may save on personnel costs since lower levels of professional preparation can be used to justify reducing salaries. However, as discussed in Chapter 3, in the United States the master's degree has its allures. It may prove to be the case that library boards with a critical mass of members who have their own master's degrees, such as the MBA or M.Ed., may see holders of such degrees as being more desirable for a director's position than possessors of a voluntary state certification based on accumulating a minimum number of community college credits or successfully completing a number of online continuing education modules.

Recent suggestions by library leaders to consider lower levels of professional preparation will be discussed in the section dealing with the substantial practitioner share of responsibility for a number of the problems afflicting librarian professionalism (below). In dealing with the liability of ALA it should be sufficient to note that the national cultures of Canada and the United States yet equate professionalism with an appropriate education at the master's level, e.g., MBA, MSW, M.Ed., etc.

Distinct Cognate Areas

The author's answer to Gorman's question, "Can the American Library Association and the LIS schools work together to produce a national core curriculum?" is, "No, not for the entire, diverse, and cobbled-together field of library and information studies." Library studies and information studies are distinct cognate areas that require equally distinct core courses, although one or two such offerings, such as an introductory course on reference and online resources, may be sufficiently "tweaked" to serve both sectors.

It is to be recalled that many programs of library and information studies are small by academic standards (Hildreth and Koenig 2002). In consequence, the growth of information courses over the years within such programs has resulted in an "information-homogenized" education as a means of attempting to address the needs of a larger spectrum of potential employers or program graduates. By declaring, albeit erroneously, that all library problems, or at least all library problems of any significance, are really information issues to be resolved by information theory, educators can justify enrolling librarians in generic courses and thereby create the curriculum "room" to concentrate on elective courses in their own areas of interest. Although cataloging or knowledge organization does have a predominant information component, most academic, public, and school library issues are more related to education and learning than information provision.

What's in a Name?

As discussed in Chapter 5, the 2005 presentation to the annual conference of the Association for Library and Information Science

Education (ALISE) by John Leslie King, dean of the School of Information of the University of Michigan, was a particularly confrontational challenge to ALA's historic right to set its own standards for accrediting programs of professional education. In that presentation, King argued that "the notion that inclusion or exclusion of the word 'library' from the names of our schools signifies something important about what's really going on inside our schools is just plain wrong." King also asserted that "people change names for good reasons, usually to signify something important to them . . . we are wasting a lot of valuable energy and effort squabbling over this because of some baseless assumptions about what it all means" (King 2005, 16).

Briefly stated, King's dismissal of the value of names in North American, particularly American culture, represents either a disingenuous attempt to avoid facing the critical importance to the culture of such names and definitions or, more charitably, it demonstrates an ignorance of the findings of other academic fields. Such ignorance reflects what the author has termed *incommensurability* or "the perceived inability to communicate effectively with one another because of a lack of common standards for meaning and other shared cultural foundations" (Crowley 2005, 204). Incommensurability is not "baseless"; it is a fundamental barrier against understanding.

If King defined himself as a librarian, it is likely he would know at a gut level the importance of "library" on campuses and in communities. On a more theoretical basis a reading of Seymour Martin Lipset's *American Exceptionalism: A Double-Edged Sword* would remind him that in a nation defined by a common creed—not the common history of European countries—words and definitions are incredibly important. In Lipset's words, "American values encourage concern for 'correctness,' both on and off campus, by the right as well as the left. Both are more moralistic, insistent on absolute standards, than their ideological compeers elsewhere in the developed world" (1996, 207). "Information" simply does not equal "library." Period.

Of course, the lack of equivalence also works against librarians defining "information" as "library." Information supporters may well be aware of the observation of Jonathan R. Cole, the provost who closed down Columbia University's School of Library Service, that the very word "library" in a program name was a barrier to recruiting leading information scholars (Cole 1990, 29). At the risk of reductionism, it is a "sauce for the goose, sauce for the gander" reality. If "library" can represent a strong negative for information advocates, "information" can and most certainly does have the same impact on quite a few "library" supporters.

While it would be foolish to demand that information faculty re-store "library" to all the names of programs accredited by ALA, it might be a reasonable, if less attractive alternative to the library com-munity, if all information programs were required to situate profes-sional library education in a school or department of library studies, library science, or librarianship, located within the college or school of information.

Language, Library, and the Needs of a National Culture

Both the national cultures of Canada and the United States share the universal cultural attribute of being based on symbols (Samovar, Porter, and McDaniel 2007, 28). Those who have spent years in pro-viding library service and helping to bring libraries into existence can provide a wealth of anecdotal evidence to back up the findings of OCLC (*Perceptions* 2005) and the Public Agenda Foundation (2006) that the word "library" is both a symbol that helps form a national culture and is defined more as an idea involving reading and learning than as a conception of information provision. During his years with the Alabama Public Library Service, the author once discussed the matter with the chair of a south Alabama library board who said, "Around these parts, the equation is God, motherhood, pecan pie, and the public library," and pointed out his belief that the library was so important a symbol that a municipality could not consider itself a "real city" without it.

ALA's regulatory capture by information educators is particularly problematic in the current age of information self-service. The mis-match between information instruction and library reality resulting from the misapplication of the information lens has increasingly ham-pered the ability of ALA-accredited programs to prepare professionals to assist in resolving the priority societal problems formerly addressed by the "old" library science—human learning and reading. To secure the future of librarian professionalism by making it essential to ef-forts to address these problems, the erroneous information homoge-nization process needs to be reversed. A library core curriculum has to be put in place with room for the new courses required to address pressing societal concerns. To help meet the public's expectations that libraries are sources of lifelong learning, new or revised core offerings are needed in such critical areas as "Libraries and Human Learning" and "Libraries and Reading." Electives such as "Libraries and Community Programming" should be made available to assist aspiring librarians in addressing the new realities of a learning culture.

The roles of educators in helping librarianship thrive as a twenty-first-century profession will be further discussed below. Here it will be noted that an ALA stipulation that the different cognate areas of "library" and "information" require separate core courses designed to provide students with a relevant education would simply recognize that a unitary approach to teaching library and information studies is no longer realistic. If properly implemented, students unsure of where they would like to work will increasingly graduate with dual majors. Obviously, such requirements will minimize the number of electives that can be taken and, as in the past, accommodations will need to be made for the area of school librarianship. However, if designed through a collaborative effort involving the library and information professional communities, in addition to educators in ALA-accredited programs, courses developed for the different cores, if periodically updated, should provide more targeted and relevant professional library and information educations.

Recommendations for ALA

To encapsulate the author's recommendations for ALA, the association should

1. broaden the current definition of the field of library and information studies to include the education, learning, and reading concerns of librarianship;
2. require programs which have dropped the word "library" from their titles to provide alternate organizational recognition of the independence of the field of librarianship through establishing a school or department of library studies, library science, or librarianship within the transformed college or school of information;
3. support education for both the "library" and "information" cognate areas through requiring separate core courses and mandating that programs offer the possibility of dual majors;

4. institute new required courses to support the librarian's learning roles, such as "Libraries and Human Learning" and "Libraries and Reading"; and

5. encourage electives such as "Libraries and Community Programming," a course that might graduate to core status as librarians in communities and on campuses adopt the "programming as learning" philosophy.

EDUCATORS IN ALA-ACCREDITED PROGRAMS

The Limitations of Communication

The reality that many ALA-accredited programs are currently providing a required information education that is largely irrelevant to many of the fundamental concerns of academic, public, and school libraries, does not result from poor communication. It is a situation that derives from the inappropriate application of a theoretical lens (Wilson 1983)—in this case the information lens—to library realities. More problematically, as is often the case in many organizations, it is also a matter of irresolvable value differences (Robbins 2003, 400), wherein faculty insist on defining library as information and library practitioners resist such an inappropriate categorization. Unfortunately, the inapplicability of the "information lens" to numerous library contexts has simply made irrelevant much of the education offered to future librarians, particularly in the mandated information courses so often prescribed within ALA-accredited programs. To borrow the words of communication theorist Stephen P. Robbins, in his text *Organizational Behavior*, the cumulative efforts of information educators to convince aspiring librarians that they are truly information specialists have, to a large extent, only served to "crystallize and reinforce [the] differences" (2003, 400) between often irrelevant information theory and the needs of library practice.

"Information" Control of the Educational Agenda

Over the last several decades the information faculty who control so many of the ALA-accredited programs have educated new practitioners on the erroneous premise that librarianship, as a subordinate component of information science, is essentially a profession devoted to information provision. In the process, these educators have succeeded in temporarily suppressing a well-established professional philosophy holding that academic, public, and school librarianship, as opposed to corporate and research information science, is primarily a profession committed to facilitating both formal education and lifelong learning.

As discussed in Chapter 3 and elsewhere, the decades-long transformation from librarianship to information science was partly an effort to distance information faculty from the admittedly low status accorded librarianship on university campuses; an attempt to safeguard the future of ALA-accredited programs in research universities by capturing education for an emerging global information market; and the means of attracting to ALA-accredited programs potential faculty stars who viewed "library work" with disdain. In addition, it also served as a justification for hiring such faculty, many of who were theorists and researchers with little or no experience working in libraries or even corporate information centers.

The early years of this information transformation, clearly beneficial for some faculty, also seemed to promise a wider spectrum of employment possibilities for students. In addition, the definition of library as primarily an information provider and librarian as information subordinate, clearly inapplicable in a number of contexts, could usually be finessed by faculty with library experience who retained an understanding of what was really required for a successful career in librarianship. The strength of the co-cultures then shared by practitioners and researchers was such that faculty teaching and researching in programs offering the ALA-accredited master's degree were often committed to making their instruction relevant to practitioner realities despite having to use fashionable, if irrelevant, information models.

However, as noted in Chapter 3, the gradual replacement of master's degree practitioners turned library faculty with Ph.D. theorists, often with little experience in libraries or information centers, professors who could be defined as academic careerists without "real-world" points of view, demonstrated the loss of the vitally important shared co-culture (Samovar, Porter, and McDaniel 2007, 11) that had smoothed over so many of the information irrelevancies to insure a more useful education for future practitioners. The growing loss of this shared identity changed the status of some educators in the eyes of practitioners; they went from being perceived as senior colleagues with a successful library past to mere inexperienced academic theorists, perhaps even unsuitable interlopers, who lack library histories, professional values, and commitments to service.

For pragmatic reasons the author expects that practitioners, who understand that the divide between librarian and information specialist is not total, that sometimes information specialists facilitate learning and that many librarians also provide information as a secondary responsibility, will prefer that ALA continue accrediting the awkwardly joined field of library and information studies. Nonetheless, in view of the ongoing dispute regarding the negative effects on librarians of the current information primacy, it is expected that library practitioner communities will insist on working with educators and the ALA accreditation structure to come up with a revised definition of the field in order to secure a more relevant professional education.

TEACHING AND RESEARCHING IN A HYBRID FIELD

Giving Up Illusions

The ability of faculty in ALA-accredited programs to take a leadership role in the preservation and extension of librarian professionalism is directly related to their willingness to give up cherished information illusions. The first such illusion is the mistaken belief that librarianship is a mere legacy that has been absorbed into information science. The reality is that librarianship is a long-established and still vibrant field whose theoretical needs have been ignored by those who see it as merely a small part of the information universe. Recognition that LIS yet remains a hybrid field brings with it the responsibility that the ALA-endorsed programs will need to insure that they employ an adequate number of "library" faculty who are capable of teaching and researching in librarianship's core areas of learning, reading, and, yes, information.

The reader is reminded that circumstances led the author to follow twenty-three years of library practice with a doctorate in higher education and a dissertation on the research university library. Such studies conveyed the reality that, for decades, the university world has been attempting to save money through merging academic units, including those offering ALA-accredited master's degrees. Looking at such programs via the "higher education lens" provided to him by Ohio University, the author sees quite a deal of validity in the aphorism that "information science without librarianship is communication, and librarianship without information science is education." Using this rubric, a strong case can be made that a transformed "information school," a program that has reduced or eliminated its support for educating librarians to help the Canadian and American cultures address programs of lifelong learning and reading, is arguably a subset of communication and should be treated as such.

This explanation, as unacceptable as she may find it, may well be the answer to the complaint of noted information scholar Marcia J. Bates that the academic world has not endorsed her ambitious claims for the supremacy of what she sees as the education, information, and communication "meta-fields." In a recent posting on JESSE, the LIS educator electronic discussion list, Bates (2007) chastises the larger academic world for not adopting information science's expansive definition of its intellectual domain. A reasonable explanation for this lack of institutional support for information science would be that the university world, whose leaders are at least as intelligent as most "information science" and "library studies" faculty, seriously considered the assumptions of information science, compared its claim for jurisdiction with those of the already established fields of communications and education, noted the considerable overlap, and questioned why it should be given a leadership role—or even a place—on campus.

Theorizing for Lifecycle Librarianship

People use reading for a variety of purposes throughout their lifetime. As part of its broad-based consideration, what may be termed the "Canadian School" of reading research has even theorized successfully on the value of "series books" in encouraging youth to read (Ross, McKechnie, and Rothbauer 2006, 83–85). The decade-long explosion in reading resulting from the Harry Potter series is but the most publicized example of this phenomenon.

Lately, Dominican University graduate students working as assistants and clerks in local public libraries have been delivering presentations in the author's classes on how libraries have been utilizing electronic ways of encouraging learning and reading. Online gaming competitions held in public libraries are now providing a range of benefits for youth, summarized by Kelly Czarnecki as encouraging "important social and educational skills including interacting with peers, adults, and family members; becoming team players, and sharpening their problem-solving and literacy skills" (2007, 34). These students have also found that providing hardcopy and electronic books and journals related to the game being played during a library-sponsored competition can and does result in increased circulation and reading by teens previously deemed to be nonreaders. This anecdotal evidence parallels the more research-oriented findings of Kurt Squire and Constance Steinkuehler (2005).

Exploring and using the learning benefits of gaming in libraries fits into the concept of *lifecycle librarianship*. This represents a paradigm or model for librarianship that has been addressed by the author from several podiums (Crowley 2007). Lifecycle librarianship should be seen as a reformulation and updating of library theory based on cooperatively implementing the best practices found in twenty-first-century academic, public, and school libraries. The concept provides an organizing principle for envisioning and cooperatively planning how libraries of all types can provide services to users, patrons, and customers throughout their lifetimes, a process that can be short-handed as "from the lapsit to the nursing home."

The development of the lifecycle approach by practitioners, the analysis of its implementation by faculty theorists, and its encouragement by ALA and state and federal funding sources, can enhance the capabilities of libraries to contribute to solving the learning and reading issues of Canadian and American cultures. In the process it (a) provides an updated justification for professional librarianship in a world where increasing information self-service is eliminating the role of information intermediary; (b) confirms the value of an education relevant to such purposes; (c) supports the worth of developing useful theory from professional practice (Crowley 2005) to guide library professionals; and, in the end, (d) justifies the value of library practice and theory from the levels of local communities and schools to the more rarified heights of research universities.

To achieve these ends, ALA-accredited programs will need to possess the knowledge base and the expertise to teach and theorize for professional librarianship that has been suppressed in recent years in the unsuccessful effort to achieve information dominance in the higher education arena. Until the support of learning and reading can be restored to the central role in library studies, and "home-grown"

Ph.D.s can graduate in substantial numbers from the ALA-accredited system, it may be necessary to recruit scholars from colleges of education and others who possess the necessary qualifications, in the same way that the programs recruited information scholars in earlier years.

Recommendations for Educators

1. Cooperate in the process of broadening the definition of library and information studies to insure representation of librarianship's learning and reading commitments.
2. Insure an appropriate organizational recognition of the distinct field or cognate area of librarianship within the structure of ALA-accredited programs. Where "library" has been dropped from program name, degrees should be offered through a school or department of library studies. Avoid dropping "library" in the future since the action removes a recognizable "brand" that helps distinguish the cognate area of information science from the better-entrenched field of communication.
3. Recognize that library studies cannot be dismissed as a mere legacy but is a vibrant field capable of meeting educational, learning, reading, and cultural needs that cannot be adequately addressed by information studies. At a minimum, treat librarianship as a separate cognate area.
4. Meet the responsibility of providing an appropriate foundational education for librarians and information specialists alike by providing—and regularly reviewing—separate systems of core courses for the distinct fields of librarianship and information studies.
5. Develop appropriate research agendas to support both library studies and information studies.
6. Educate future LIS faculty equipped to teach and research librarianship's learning and reading commitments.
7. Insure that the faculty hiring process secures the services of scholars and educators committed to supporting both the library studies and information studies cognate areas of the rather cumbersomely named field of library and information studies.

PRACTITIONERS

Two Views of Library Practitioners

In the late 1990s, as the author was completing his transition from practitioner to Dominican University educator, he found himself commiserating with a serving state librarian—a friend from his previous professional life—who described how an extensive and expensive effort to encourage public librarians to adopt a marketing approach to serving their communities had ended in failure. When asked by the author why the endeavor had failed, the state librarian grew reflective and raised the possibility that the librarians of his state were underestimating their ability to succeed in meeting new challenges. The discussion was far-ranging and even addressed the possibility that the continuing use of the Myers-Briggs Type Indicator in library circles had wrongly convinced a number of librarians that they were too introverted (Rubin 2004, 474) to thrive in contemporary contexts.

During the previous decade a threat to federal library funding arose just as the author was taking up a position as the administrator of a regional multitype library cooperative in Indiana, one of nine such in existence at the time. Since federal dollars were absolutely essential to supporting the cooperative's programs of service, the author was asked by his board to train local academic, public, and school librarians on how they and their supporters could communicate the value of library services to the state's congressional representatives and federal senators. Following the suggestion of the then-serving state librarian the author soon after offered variations of the workshop around the state.

At the beginning of each workshop, the author asked about the political experience of those present and inevitably found that half the audience or more expressed considerable anxiety about working with legislators. After spending several hours in learning a spectrum of proven techniques—which the author largely borrowed from League of Women Voters pamphlets—the workshop attendees left for home with a bit more confidence. Within a year, after applying these approaches on local, state, and national levels, many of the self-defined political neophytes proved themselves to be far better political communicators than the author could ever aspire to be (Crowley 1988).

In short, only their self-doubt and lack of training had kept a significant number of Indiana librarians from demonstrating just how well they could communicate the library message. It is a similar lack of practitioner confidence that the author believes must be addressed in the hard but productive work necessary to insure the future of professional librarianship.

Whose Fault Is It?

Ultimately, since ALA is the accrediting agency for programs of library and information education, it is the responsibility of the association's membership to insure that the system is providing relevant professional education. This obligation is ongoing since human systems are not self-correcting and need regular attention. Complicating matters is the reality that the ALA bureaucracy and system of accreditation has become a case study of regulatory capture by the programs it is supposed to oversee. Fortunately, the situation can still be reversed. The rules under which academics must conduct their professional lives and which encourage such capture are easy to discover (Crowley 2005). Once practitioners learn these rules and combine such understandings with their knowledge of the education librarians need to provide first-rate service to their communities, the object of a relevant professional education ought to be achievable. The only obvious negative is the fact that working with academics and the ALA bureaucracy to reform the present accreditation structure is likely to take longer than convincing the U.S. Congress to preserve and expand federal library funding.

What Not To Do

The one thing that practitioners absolutely have to avoid in the process of safeguarding professional librarianship is the temptation to remove the official standard of a master's degree from an ALA-accredited program. Recent suggestions to consider lowering the level of education for new librarians to the bachelor's degree level, such as that advanced by George Needham at the Thinking Ahead Symposium 2006 (Needham 2007) are useful only if the possibility is immediately dismissed. The author is a twenty-year friend of Needham, and is well aware of the thoughtful approach to library issues taken by this former executive director of the Public Library Association, Michigan

State Librarian, and current OCLC vice president for Member Services. In consequence, he would find it out of character if Needham had brought up this option for other than discussion purposes.

The possibility of reducing the educational requirements for professional librarianship seems to be a spur-of-the-moment suggestion with profoundly negative implications that have not been sufficiently considered. It certainly did not seem to be supported by the findings of such recent studies as *The Future of Human Resources in Canadian Libraries* (Ingles 2005) and *The Next Library Leadership: Attributes of Academic and Public Library Directors* (Hernon, Powell, and Young 2003).

In general, the possibility of lowering educational standards in order to pay librarians less has particular appeal to three significant categories within the library community. These include library practitioners and trustees who

1. live in those areas of the United States and Canada where a long history of minimum funding and a lack of locally available professional education (Helmick and Swigger 2006, 54) developed what can only be described as a self-defensive rejection of the very professionalism that could not be easily secured. That this mindset continues in a period where respectable undergraduate and graduate degrees, including degrees in LIS, are now available via the Internet to even the most geographically isolated, suggests that local library communities may have fallen short on their responsibility to educate voters on the value of quality library service directed by educated and committed professionals;

2. value existing library service far more than the enhanced possibilities offered through the presence of professionally educated librarians. This mindset rejects creative ways (interlibrary cooperation agreements, shared directorships, etc.) to secure needed librarian professionalism;

3. fail in their positions of trust because their own unwillingness to engage with their communities to market relevant services and advocate for adequate funding has negatively impacted the budgets of their libraries. That so many "library leaders" fall into this category is the not-so-secret shame of the profession.

It is too little recalled by those who advocate setting the educational bar for professional librarianship at the level of the bachelor's degree that they are arguing for a lower standard than the one that existed in 1950. In the middle of the last century professional librarians possessed a fifth-year bachelor's degree, earned after achieving a B.A. with an extensive arts and sciences component. Dumbing down the qualification for a beginning librarian to less than the level of the last century, in addition to destroying academic librarianship, would send the worst possible signal to communities which see the JD, MBA, or MSW as accepted professional standards. Since librarians have failed in their responsibility to achieve compulsive licensure, arguments to emulate the career path of licensed teachers are fallacious. Librarianship is based on helping to address formal and informal lifelong learning and reading in a variety of contexts, with a secondary information provision component. In consequence, while narrowing the preparation of beginning librarians may save employers money by lowering starting salaries, it is equally likely to reinforce the "anyone can be a librarian" perception that the library community itself has encouraged through its embarrassing lack of mandatory licensure.

What To Do

In collaboration with the ALA bureaucracy and sympathetic educators in ALA-accredited programs, practitioners need, first and foremost, to adopt the affirmative agenda of *lifecycle librarianship*. The title of this model is not important. If academic, public, and school library professionals feel the need to rename a concept of library service that begins with the learning, story, and reading needs of young children and concludes with the continuing learning interests, electronic or otherwise, of their great-grandparents, so much the better. As a pragmatist and former library public relations representative, the author is more concerned with successful actions than with credit.

Library professionals need to experiment with a variety of approaches to formal and informal collaboration among academic, public, and school librarians to help solve the learning and reading issues facing American and Canadian cultures. Such cooperation should include a strong marketing component, identification of best practices, and funding to diffuse knowledge of the most valuable achievements.

In particular there must be successful cooperative planning and the provision of workshop training in effective approaches for currently serving professionals, as well as the mandating of relevant courses for aspiring librarians in ALA-accredited programs. Strong and sustained efforts to demonstrate to current and potential library users that any and all reading, specifically including reading for pleasure, has beneficial learning effects will be absolutely necessary.

Recommendations for Practitioners

Once the preceding is in place, the author would suggest the following actions for the various library practitioner communities:

1. support efforts to change the definition of library and information studies to recognize the continuing roles of academic, public, and school libraries in helping to address national problems with learning and reading;
2. recognize that new, library-oriented textbooks are needed. At the present time, information publications have a greater market than library publications as texts for ALA-accredited programs. Members should require ALA to seek grant funding to commission and subsidize, for a limited period of time, a number of low-cost publications on the library's roles in support of education, learning, and reading, including textbooks in hard-copy and electronic formats. To avoid "capture" by the ALA publishing bureaucracy, the commissioning and issuance of such works should be negotiated with a spectrum of library and information publishers, including ALA;
3. develop national, state/provincial, and local-level marketing and public relations campaigns to emphasize the library as a valuable resource for maintaining and expanding the lifelong learning opportunities and reading skills of Americans and Canadians. Such campaigns should specifically include programming and other cultural learning opportunities. The proposed ALA/Canadian Library Association campaigns, which in the broadest sense of the term will be political in nature, need to keep in mind that research has found that winning strategies for getting public attention and legislative action have a
   a. common concept around which to gather "solutions and ideas";

b. "solution at hand [that] is simple, easily understood, and strengthened with personal anecdotes";
c. common name (Christie 2005).

In the author's opinion, the common *concept* for a successful library campaign is the need to support lifelong learning, reading, and literacy; the *solution* is the library and librarian, and the *common name* is lifecycle librarianship. As a former PR person with the New York Public Library, the author is amused to think about the possibilities for developing and marketing a campaign on a variation of "Libraries: Learning and reading for a lifetime—It's educational, profitable, and fun."

A Vision of The Future of The Professional Librarian

In the American and Canadian federal systems, a planned approach to serving the lifelong learning and reading needs of local residents, students, and faculty members, using applicable technologies as they become available, represents an achievable goal that can substantially enhance the prospects for professional librarianship. Even the future of corporate and research information and knowledge managers can be improved in an environment where people increasingly look to library professionals for assistance. A first-class librarian as "library/learning/reading intermediary" who catches youth at an impressionable age will actually train customers, patrons, and users to be on the lookout for similar assistance in more adult environments. Even in the secular university or commercial marketplace there remains much truth in the old Jesuit aphorism, "Give me a child until he is seven and I will give you the man [or woman]."

By now readers should understand that the author, who does not know all their professional contexts, has not attempted a step-by-step "cookbook" for solving all the problems facing librarian professionalism. As noted at several points, the author is a pragmatist, and pragmatists are wary of claiming to know all the answers. In this context it is worthwhile to recall an observation of John Dewey, advanced in his nearly unreadable but incredibly valuable *Logic: The Theory of Inquiry,* to the effect that *no* theory that was really worth anything was ever proven to be true "in the form in which it was originally presented nor without very considerable revisions and modifications" (Dewey and Boydston 1991, 512). In these limited pages the author, under the auspices of Beta Phi Mu and its Editorial Board, has provided ALA (and Canadian Library Association), educators in ALA-accredited programs, and academic, public, and school library practitioners, with a statement of the problem, its relevant history, a range of analyses and definitions, and a few recommendations for change. He now challenges the reader to do something with them.

In helping to safeguard and justify the future of the professional librarian, it would simply be the pragmatic thing to do.

References

American Library Association. 1992. *Standards for Accreditation of Master's Programs in Library & Information Studies.* Chicago: Office for Accreditation, American Library Association.

Association of College and Research Libraries. 2001. Statement on the terminal professional degree for academic librarians. http://www.ala.org/ala/acrl/acrlstandards/statementterminal.htm (accessed July 13, 2007).

Bates, Marcia J. 1999. The invisible substrate of information science. *Journal of the American Society for Information Science* 50, no. 12 (October): 1043–1050.

———. 2007. Re: Buffalo & LIS role in universities. JESSE Open Lib/Info Sci Education Forum, March 2, 2007. http://listserv.utk.edu/cgi-bin/wa?A2=ind0703&L=JESSE&P=R2427&I=-3 (accessed July 22, 2007).

British Columbia Teacher-Librarian's Association. 2006. *25th Annual Survey of Working and Learning Conditions: Report of Findings.* British Columbia Teacher-Librarians' Association. http://bctf.ca/bctla/wlc2006.pdf (accessed April 12, 2007).

Burnaby Public Library. 2006. *Reflections: Memories from our First 50 Years—As Told by Our Patrons.* Burnaby, Canada: Burnaby Public Library.

Buschman, John E. 2003. *Dismantling the Public Sphere: Situating and Sustaining Librarianship in the Age of the New Public Philosophy.* Westport, CT: Libraries Unlimited.

Christie, Kathy. 2005. Critical mass. *Phi Delta Kappan* 86, no. 7 (March): 485–486. Wilson Web. http://relayweb.hwwilsonweb.com/hww/results/external_link_maincontentframe.jhtml?_DARGS=/hww/results/results_common.jhtml.9 (accessed April 12, 2007).

Cole, Jonathan R. 1990. *Report of the Provost on the School of Library Service at Columbia.* New York: Columbia University in the City of New York.

Cronin, Blaise. 2000. Accreditation: Retool it or kill it. *Library Journal* (15 June): 54.

———. 2001. The dreaded "L" word. *Library Journal* (15 March): 58.

Crowley, Bill. 1988. A blueprint for legislative activism: Forging Indiana's lobbying network; a "how to" guide from a sister state. *Ohio Media Spectrum* 40, no. 4 (winter): 5–8.

———. 2004. Just another field? *Library Journal* (1 November): 44–46.

———. 2005. *Spanning the Theory-Practice Divide in Library and Information Science.* Lanham, MD: Scarecrow Press.

——. 2006. Suicide prevention: Safeguarding the future of the professional librarian. *Library Administration & Management* 20, 2 (spring): 75–80.

——. 2007. Don't let Google and the pennypinchers get you down: Defending (or redefining) libraries and librarianship in the age of technology. Presentation at the British Columbia Library Association Annual Conference 2007: Beyond 20/20: Envisioning the Future, Burnaby, British Columbia (Canada). http://eprints.rclis.org/archive/00009526 (accessed July 10, 2007).

Crowley, Bill, and Deborah Ginsberg. 2003. Intracultural reciprocity, information ethics, and the survival of librarianship in the 21st century. In *Ethics and Electronic Information: A Festschrift for Stephen Almagno,* ed. Tom Medina and Barbara Rockenbach, 94–107. Jefferson, NC: McFarland & Company.

——. 2005. Professional values: Priceless. *American Libraries* (January): 52–55.

Czarnecki, Kelly. 2007. A revolution in library service: Gaming is more than just a lure into the library. *School Library Journal* 53, no. 5 (May): 34–35.

Dal Bo, Ernesto. 2006. Regulatory capture: A review. *Oxford Review of Economic Policy* 22, no. 2 (summer): 203–225.

Dewey, John, and Jo Ann Boydston. 1991. *The Later Works, 1925–1953. Volume 12: 1938 Logic: The Theory of Inquiry.* Carbondale: Southern Illinois University Press.

Gorman, Michael. 2004. Whither library education? *New Library World* 105, nos. 1204/1205 (September): 376–380.

Great Britain. Parliament. House of Commons. Culture, Media and Sport Committee. 2005a. *Public Libraries.* Vol. 1. London: Stationary Office. http://www.publications.parliament.uk/pa/cm200405/cmselect/cmcumeds/81/81i.pdf (accessed January 27, 2007).

——. 2005b. *Public Libraries.* Vol. 2. London: Stationary Office. http://www.publications.parliament.uk/pa/cm200405/cmselect/cmcumeds/81/81i.pdf (accessed January 27, 2007).

Hamilton-Pennell, Christine. 2003. Public library standards: A review of standards and guidelines from the 50 states of the U.S. for the Colorado, Mississippi and Hawaii state libraries. Mosaic Knowledge Works. http://www.tsl.state.tx.us/plstandards/minstand.html (accessed July 11, 2007).

Hardin, Garrett. 1968. The tragedy of the commons. *Science* 162 (13 December): 1243–1248.

Haycock, Ken. 2003. *The Crisis in Canada's School Libraries: The Case for Reform and Re-Investment: A Report for the Association of Canadian Publishers.* Toronto: Association of Canadian Publishers.

Helmick, Catherine, and Keith Swigger. 2006. Core competencies of library practitioners. *Public Libraries* 45, no. 2 (March/April): 54–69.

Hernon, Peter, Ronald R. Powell, and Arthur P. Young. 2003. *The Next Library Leadership: Attributes of Academic and Public Library Directors.* Westport, CT: Libraries Unlimited.

Hildreth, Charles R., and Michael Koenig. 2002. Organizational realignment of LIS programs in academia: From independent standalone units to incorporated programs. *Journal of Education for Library and Information Science* 43, no. 2 (spring): 126–133.

Ingles, Ernest Boyce. 2005. *The Future of Human Resources in Canadian Libraries*.8Rs Canadian Library Human Resource Study.

King, John Leslie. 2005. Stepping Up: Shaping the Future of the Field. Plenary Session 3 presentation, January 14 at the ALISE 2005 Conference. dLIST. http://dlist.sir.arizona.edu/739 (accessed June 27, 2007).

Lipset, Seymour Martin. 1996. *American Exceptionalism: A Double-Edged Sword.* New York: Norton.

McCabe, Ronald B. 2001. *Civic Librarianship: Renewing the Social Mission of the Public Library.* Lanham, MD: Scarecrow Press.

Needham, George. 2006. Outline of presentation "The Library Education Conundrum" at the *Thinking Ahead Symposium.* Attachment to email to author, January 9, 2007.

Ontario Library Association, Queen's University (Kingston, Ont.), People for Education. 2006. *School Libraries & Student Achievement in Ontario.* Toronto: Ontario Library Association. http://www.accessola.com/osla/graphics/eqao_pfe_study_2006.pdf (accessed April 10, 2007).

Parker, Wendy L., Ward Bower, and Jane Weissman. 2002. Costs and benefits of practitioner certification or licensure for the solar industry. In IEEE Photovoltaic Specialists Conference. *Conference Record of the Twenty-Ninth IEEE Photovoltaic Specialists Conference, 2002: Hyatt Regency, New Orleans, Louisiana, May 19-24, 2002.* Piscataway, NJ: IEEE. http://www.irecusa.org/fileadmin/user_upload/WorkforceDevelopmentDocs/CertificationorLicensure.pdf (accessed July 13, 2007).

Perceptions of Libraries and Information Resources: A Report to the OCLC Membership. 2005. Principal contributors, Cathy De Rosa et al. Dublin, OH: OCLC Online Computer Library Center. http://www.oclc.org/reports/2005perceptions.htm (accessed September 22, 2006).

Public Agenda Foundation. 2006. *Long Overdue: A Fresh Look at Public Attitudes About Libraries in the 21st Century.* New York: Public Agenda.

Robbins, Stephen P. 2003. *Organizational Behavior,* 10th ed. Upper Saddle River, NJ: Prentice Hall.

Ross, Catherine Sheldrick, Lynne (E.F.) McKechnie, and Paulette M. Rothbauer. 2006. *Reading Matters: What the Research Reveals about Reading, Libraries, and Community.* Westport, CT: Libraries Unlimited.

Rubin, Richard E. 2004. *Foundations of Library and Information Science,* 2nd ed. New York: Neal-Schuman.

Samovar, Larry A., Richard E. Porter, and Edwin R. McDaniel. 2007. *Communication Between Cultures,* 6th ed. Belmont, CA: Thomson Wadsworth.

Squire, Kurt, and Constance Steinkuehler. 2005. Meet the gamers. *Library Journal* 130, no. 7 (15 April): 38–41.

Wiegand, Wayne A. 2001. Missing the real story: Where library and information science fails the library profession. In *The Readers' Advisor's Companion,* ed. Kenneth D. Shearer and Robert Burgin, 7–14. Englewood, CO: Libraries Unlimited.

————. 2003. To reposition a research agenda: What American Studies can teach the LIS community about the library in the life of the user. *Library Quarterly* 73, no. 4 (October): 369–382.

————. 2005. Critiquing the curriculum. *American Libraries* 36, no. 1 (January): 58, 60–61.

Williams, Patrick. 1988. *The American Public Library and the Problem of Purpose.* Contributions in librarianship and information science, no. 62. New York: Greenwood Press.

Wilson, Patrick. 1983. *Second-Hand Knowledge: An Inquiry into Cognitive Authority.* Westport, CT: Greenwood Press.

Bibliography

Abbott, Andrew. 1988. *The System of Professions: An Essay on the Division of Expert Labor*. Chicago: University of Chicago Press.

ACT, Inc. 2006. *Reading Between the Lines: What the ACT Reveals About College Readiness in Reading*. Iowa City, Iowa: ACT. http://www.act.org/path/policy/pdf/reading_report.pdf (accessed August 1, 2007).

American Library Association. 1992. *Standards for Accreditation of Master's Programs in Library & Information Studies*. Chicago, IL: Office for Accreditation, American Library Association.

Apostle, Richard, and Boris Raymond. 1997. *Librarianship and the Information Paradigm*. Lanham, MD: Scarecrow Press.

Argyris, Chris. 1999. Tacit knowledge and management. In *Tacit Knowledge in Professional Practice: Researcher and Practitioner Perspectives*, ed. Robert J. Sternberg and Joseph A. Horvath, 123–140. Mahwah, NJ: Lawrence Erlbaum Associates.

Aspray, William. 1999. Command and control, documentation, and library science: The origins of information science at the University of Pittsburgh. *IEEE Annals of the History of Computing* 21, no. 4 (October–December): 4–20.

Association of College and Research Libraries. 2001. Statement on the terminal professional degree for academic librarians. http://www.ala.org/ala/acrl/acrlstandards/statementterminal.htm (accessed July 13, 2007).

Association of Universities and Colleges of Canada. *Directory of Canadian Universities* http://oraweb.aucc.ca/showdcu.html (accessed December 28, 2006).

Augst, Thomas, and Wayne Wiegand. 2001. *The Library as an Agency of Culture*. Lawrence, KS: American Studies. Reprint of the fall 2001 issue of *American Studies* 42, no. 3.

Barzun, Jacques. 1978. The professions under siege. *Harper's* (October): 61–66, 68.

Bates, Marcia J. 1999. The invisible substrate of information science. *Journal of the American Society for Information Science* 50, no. 12 (October): 1043–1050.

———. 2004. Information science at the University of California at Berkeley in the 1960s: A memoir of student days. *Library Trends* 52, no. 4 (spring): 683–701.

Becher, Tony. 1989. *Academic Tribes and Territories: Intellectual Enquiry and the Cultures of Disciplines*. Buckingham, England: Society for Research into Higher Education & Open University Press.

Becker, Howard S. 1998. *Tricks of the Trade: How to Think About Your Research While You're Doing It*. Chicago: University of Chicago Press.

Berry, John N. III. 2006. Can ALA bring change? *Library Journal.* 131, no. 15 (15 September). http://www.libraryjournal.com/article/CA6370229.html (accessed February 1, 2007).

Biggs, Mary. 1985. Who/what/why should a library educator be? *Journal of Education for Library and Information Science* 25, no. 4 (spring): 262–278.

Bowles, Mark D. 1999. The information wars: Two cultures and the conflict in information retrieval, 1945–1999. in *Proceedings of the 1998 Conference on the History and Heritage of Science Information Systems,* ed. Mary Ellen Bowen, Trudi Bellardo Hahn, Robert V. Williams, 156–166. Medford, NJ: Published for the American Society for Information Science and the Chemical Heritage Foundation by Information Today.

British Columbia Teacher-Librarian's Association. 2006. *25th Annual Survey of Working and Learning Conditions: Report of Findings.* British Columbia Teacher-Librarians' Association. http://bctf.ca/bctla/wlc2006.pdf (accessed April 12, 2007).

Broady-Preston, Judith. 2006. CILIP: A twenty-first century association for the information profession? *Library Management* 27 (1/2): 48–65.

Broderick, Dorothy M. 1997. Turning library into a dirty word: A rant. *Library Journal* 122, no. 12 (July): 42–43.

Brooks, David. 2004. A polarized America. Special issue on discourse and democracy. *Hedgehog Review* 6, no. 3: 14–23. Based on the transcript of the Labrosse-Levinson Lecture delivered by David Brooks at the University of Virginia on October 20, 2004.

Buckland, Michael K. 2003. Five grand challenges for library research. *Library Trends* 51, no. 4 (spring): 675–686.

Budd, John M. 2004. Relevance: Language, semantics, philosophy. *Library Trends* 52, no. 3 (winter): 447–462.

Burger, Leslie. 2007. Changing library education. Instructional program transformation is key to the profession. *American Libraries* 38, no. 4. (April): 5.

Burnaby Public Library. 2006. *Reflections: Memories from our First 50 Years—As Told by Our Patrons.* Burnaby, Canada: Burnaby Public Library.

Burnett, Kathleen M., and Laurie J. Bonnici. 2006. Contested terrain: Accreditation and the future of the profession of librarianship. *Library Quarterly* 76, no. 2 (April): 193–219.

Buschman, John E. 2003. *Dismantling the Public Sphere: Situating and Sustaining Librarianship in the Age of the New Public Philosophy.* Westport, CT: Libraries Unlimited.

Bush, Vannevar. 1945. As we may think. *Atlantic Monthly,* July. http://www.theatlantic.com/doc/print/194507/bush (accessed December 11, 2006).

Chandler, Susan. 2006. To thine own brand be true. *Chicago Tribune,* December 24, 2006, sec. 2 Perspective.

Chartered Institute of Library and Information Professionals (CILIP). 2004a. *Body of Professional Knowledge: Setting Out an Adaptable and Flexible Framework for Your Changing Needs.* London: Chartered Institute of Library and Information Professionals. http://www.cilip.org.uk/qualificationschartership/bpk (accessed March 7, 2007).

——. 2004b. *Certification Scheme Handbook: CILIP's Framework of Qualifications, Enhancing Opportunities, Rewarding Achievement.* London: Chartered Institute of Library and Information Professionals. http://www.cilip.org.uk/qualification schartership/FrameworkofQualifications/certification (accessed March 7, 2007).

Christie, Kathy. 2005. Critical mass. *Phi Delta Kappan.* 86, no. 7 (March): 485–486. Wilson Web. http://relayweb.hwwilsonweb.com/hww/results/external_link_ maincontentframe.jhtml?_DARGS=/hww/results/results_common.jhtml.9 (accessed April 12, 2007).

Clark, Burton R. 1987. *The Academic Life: Small Worlds, Different Worlds.* Princeton, NJ: Carnegie Foundation for the Advancement of Teaching.

Coates, Tim. 2004. *Who's in Charge? Responsibility for the Public Library Service.* London: Libri Trust.

Cochrane, Mary. 2006. FSEC supports dissolving informatics school. *University at Buffalo Reporter*, November 30, 2006. http://www.buffalo.edu/reporter/vol38/vol38n13/articles/FSEC.html (accessed April 2, 2007).

Cole, Jonathan R. 1990. *Report of the Provost on the School of Library Service at Columbia.* New York: Columbia University in the City of New York.

College Students' Perceptions of Libraries and Information Resources: A Report to the OCLC Membership. 2006. Principal contributors, Cathy De Rosa et al. Dublin, OH: OCLC Online Computer Library Center. http://www.oclc.org/reports/perceptionscollege.htm (accessed September 22, 2006).

Corcoran, Mary, Lynn Dagar, and Anthea Stratigos. 2000. The changing roles of information professionals: Excerpts from an Outsell, Inc. study. *Online* (March/April): 29–30, 32–34.

Cox, Richard J. 2006. Why survival is not enough. *American Libraries* 37, no. 6 (June/July): 42–44.

Cronin, Blaise. 1995a. Shibboleth and substance in North American library and information science education. *Libri* 45, no. 1 (March): 45–63.

——. 1995b. Cutting the Gordian knot. *Information Processing & Management* 31, no. 6 (November): 897–902.

——. 2000a. Accreditation: Retool it or kill it. *Library Journal* 125, no.11 (15 June): 54.

——. 2000b. Quis custodiet custodes? *International Journal of Information Management* 20, no. 4 (August): 311–313.

——. 2001a. The view from the trenches. *Library Journal* 126, no. 11 (15 June): 52.

——. 2001b. The dreaded "L" word. *Library Journal* 126, no. 5 (15 March): 58.

——. 2002. Holding the center while prospecting at the periphery: Domain identity and coherence in North American information studies education. *Education for Information* 20, no. 1 (March): 3–10.

Crowley, Bill. 1988. A blueprint for legislative activism: Forging Indiana's lobbying network; a "how to" guide from a sister state. *Ohio Media Spectrum* 40, no. 4 (winter): 5–8.

——. 1994. Library lobbying as a way of life. *Public Libraries* 33, no 2 (March–April): 96–98.

——. 1997. The dilemma of the librarian in Canadian higher education. *Canadian Journal of Information and Library Science* 22, no. 1 (April): 1–18.

——. 1998. Dumping the "Library." *Library Journal* 123, no. 12 (July): 48–49.

——. 1999a. Building useful theory: Tacit knowledge, practitioner reports, and the culture of LIS inquiry. *Journal of Education for Library and Information Science* 40, no. 4 (fall): 282–295.

——. 1999b. The control and direction of professional education. *Journal of the American Society for Information Science* 50, no. 12 (October): 1127–1135.

——. 2000. Tacit knowledge and quality assurance: Bridging the theory-practice divide. In *Knowledge management for the information professional*, ed. T. Kanti Srikantaiah and Michael E. D. Koenig, 205–220. Medford, NJ: Published for the American Society for Information Science by Information Today.

——. 2001. Tacit knowledge, tacit ignorance, and the future of academic librarianship. *College & Research Libraries* 62, no. 6 (November): 565–584.

——. 2003. The suicide of the public librarian. *Library Journal* 128 (15 April): 48–49.

——. 2004. Just another field? *Library Journal* 129 (1 November): 44–46.

——. 2005a. Rediscovering the history of readers advisory service. *Public Libraries* 44, no. 1 (January/February): 37–41.

——. 2005b. Save professionalism. *Library Journal* 130, no. 14 (1 September): 46–48.

——. 2005c. *Spanning the Theory-Practice Divide in Library and Information Science.* Lanham, MD: Scarecrow Press.

——. 2006. Suicide prevention. *Library Administration & Management* 20, no. 2 (spring): 75–80.

——. 2007. Don't let Google and the pennypinchers get you down: Defending (or redefining) libraries and librarianship in the age of technology. Presentation at the British Columbia Library Association Annual Conference 2007: Beyond 20/20: Envisioning the Future, Burnaby, British Columbia (Canada). http://eprints.rclis.org/archive/00009526 (accessed July 10, 2007).

Crowley, Bill, and Bill Brace. 1999. A choice of futures: Is it libraries versus information? *American Libraries* 30 (April): 76–77, 79.

Crowley, Bill, and Deborah Ginsberg. 2003. Intracultural reciprocity, information ethics, and the survival of librarianship in the 21st century. In *Ethics and Electronic Information: A Festschrift for Stephen Almagno*, ed. Tom Medina and Barbara Rockenbach, 94–107. Jefferson, NC: McFarland & Company.

——. 2005. Professional values: Priceless. *American Libraries* (January): 52–55.

Crowley, William A. Jr. 1995. A Draft Research Model of the Research University Library: Exploring the Scholar-Librarian Partnership of Jaroslav Pelikan in *The Idea of the University: A Reexamination*. PhD. diss., Ohio University.

Cuban, Larry. 1999. *How Scholars Trumped Teachers: Change Without Reform in University Curriculum, Teaching, and Research, 1890–1990.* New York: Teachers College Press.

Cunningham, Anne, and Keith Stanovich. 1998. What reading does for the mind. *American Educator* 22, nos. 1–2 (spring–summer): 1–8.

Czarnecki, Kelly. 2007. A revolution in library service: Gaming is more than just a lure into the library. *School Library Journal* 53, no. 5 (May): 34–35.

Dal Bo, Ernesto. 2006. Regulatory capture: A review. *Oxford Review of Economic Policy* 22, no. 2 (summer): 203–225.

Deane, Gary. 2003. Bridging the value gap: Getting past professional values to customer *value* in the public library. *Public Libraries* 42, no. 5 (September–October): 315–319.

Dervin, Brenda, and CarrieLynn D. Reinhard. 2006. Researchers and practitioners talk about users and each other. Making user and audience studies matter—paper 1. *Information Research* 12, no 1. (October). http://informationr.net/ir/12-1/paper286.html (accessed March 8, 2007).

Dewey, John, and Jo Ann Boydston. 1991. *The Later Works, 1925–1953. Volume 12: 1938 Logic: The Theory of Inquiry.* Carbondale: Southern Illinois University Press.

Dillon, Andrew, and April Norris. 2005. Crying wolf: An examination and reconsideration of the perception of crisis in LIS education. *Journal of Education for Library and Information Science* 46, no. 4 (fall): 280–298.

Earned degrees conferred, 2003-4. 2006. *Chronicle of Higher Education* 53, no. 1 (25 August): 22.

Ehrenhalt, Alan. 2004. Assessments: Spreading out the clout. *Governing* (April): 6, 8.

Eliot, Charles W. 1869. The new education, parts 1 and 2. *Atlantic Monthly* 23: 203–220, 356–367.

Elshtain, Jean Bethke. 2001. Jane Addams and the social claim. *Public Interest* 145 (fall): 82–92.

Faure-Grimaud, Antoine, and David Martimort. 2003. Regulatory inertia. *RAND Journal of Economics* 34, no. 3 (autumn): 413–437.

Fialkoff, Francine. 2007. Lusting after Ohio's libraries. *Library Journal* 132, no. 10 (1 June): 8.

Frickel, Scott, and Neil Gross. 2005. A general theory of scientific/intellectual movements. *American Sociological Review* 70, no. 2 (April): 204–232.

Galvin, Thomas J. 1992. The new ALA standards for accreditation: A personal perspective. *Bulletin of the American Society for Information Science* 18, no. 4 (April/May): 19–20.

Garrison Dee. 1979. *Apostles of Culture: The Public Librarian and American Society, 1876–1920.* New York: Free Press.

Gorman, G. E. 1999. The future for library science education. *Libri* 49, no. 1 (March): 1–10.

Gorman, Michael. 2000. *Our Enduring Values: Librarianship in the 21st Century.* Chicago: American Library Association.

———. 2004. Whither library education? *New Library World* 105, nos. 1204/1205 (September): 376–380.

Great Britain. Parliament. House of Commons. Culture, Media and Sport Committee. 2005a. *Public Libraries.* Vol. 1. London: Stationary Office. http://www.publications.parliament.uk/pa/cm200405/cmselect/cmcumeds/81/81i.pdf (accessed January 27, 2007).

———. 2005b. *Public Libraries.* Vol. 2. London: Stationary Office. http://www.publications.parliament.uk/pa/cm200405/cmselect/cmcumeds/81/81i.pdf (accessed January 27, 2007).

Hamilton-Pennell. Christine, 2003. Public library standards: A review of standards and guidelines from the 50 states of the U.S. for the Colorado, Mississippi and Hawaii state libraries. Mosaic Knowledge Works. http://www.tsl.state.tx.us/plstandards/minstand.html (accessed July 11, 2007).

Hardin, Garrett. 1968. The tragedy of the commons. *Science,* 162 (13 December): 1243–1248.

Hardy, Cynthia. 1996. *The Politics of Collegiality: Retrenchment Strategies in Canadian Universities.* Montreal and Kingston: McGill-Queen's University Press.

Harmon, Glynn, ed. 2006a. Introduction. The first I-conference of the I-school communities. Special section, *Bulletin of the American Society for Information Science and Technology* (April/May): 9–10.

———, ed. 2006b. The first I-Conference of the I-school communities. Special section, *Bulletin of the American Society for Information Science and Technology* (April/May): 9–23.

Harris, Michael H., and Stan A. Hannah. 1993. *Into the Future: The Foundations of Library and Information Services in the Post-Industrial Era.* Norwood, NJ: Ablex.

Haycock, Ken. 2000. The Congress on Professional Education in North America. Paper presented at the 66th IFLA Council and General Conference, Jerusalem, Israel. http://www.ifla.org/IV/ifla66/papers/146-156e.htm (accessed March 29, 2007).

———. 2003. *The Crisis in Canada's School Libraries: The Case for Reform and Re-Investment: A Report for the Association of Canadian Publishers.* Toronto: Association of Canadian Publishers.

Helmick, Catherine, and Keith Swigger. 2006. Core competencies of library practitioners. *Public Libraries* 45, no. 2 (March/April): 54–69.

Hennen, Thomas J. Jr. 2006. Hennen's American Public Library Ratings 2006. *American Libraries* 37, no. 10 (November): 40–42.

Hernon, Peter, Ronald R. Powell, and Arthur P. Young. 2003. *The Next Library Leadership: Attributes of Academic and Public Library Directors.* Westport, CT: Libraries Unlimited.

Hildreth, Charles R., and Michael Koenig. 2002. Organizational realignment of LIS programs in academia: From independent standalone units to incorporated programs. *Journal of Education for Library and Information Science* 43, no. 2 (spring): 126–133.

Ingles, Ernest Boyce. 2005. *The Future of Human Resources in Canadian Libraries.* 8Rs Canadian Library Human Resource Study.

KALIPER (Project). 2000. *Educating Library and Information Science Professionals for a New Century, the KALIPER Report.* Reston, VA: KALIPER Advisory Committee, Association for Library and Information Science Education (ALISE).

Kansas, Office of the Governor. 2006. Governor's appointees promote libraries as life-long learning resources: Sebelius appoints two, reappoints six to Southeast Regional Library System. News release, February 3, 2006. http://www.governor.ks.gov/news/NewsRelease/2006/nr-06-0203a.html (accessed December 13, 2006).

Karetzky, Stephen. 1982. *Reading Research and Librarianship: A History and Analysis.* Contributions in librarianship and information science, no. 36. Westport, CT: Greenwood Press.

Kertzer, David I. 1988. *Ritual, Politics, and Power.* New Haven: Yale University Press.

King, John Leslie. 2005. Stepping Up: Shaping the Future of the Field. Plenary Session 3 presentation, January 14 at the ALISE 2005 Conference. dLIST http:// dlist.sir.arizona.edu/739 (accessed June 27, 2007).

Koenig, Michael E. D. 1990. Buttering the toast evenly: Library school closings at Columbia and Chicago are tragic; but they don't have to signal a trend. *American Libraries* 21 (September): 723–724, 726.

Koenig, Michael E. D., and Charles Hildreth. 2002. The end of the standalone "library school." *Library Journal* 127, no. 11 (June 15): 40–41.

Krashen, Stephen D. 2004. *The Power of Reading: Insights from the Research,* 2nd ed. Westport, CT: Libraries Unlimited.

Kuhn, Thomas S. 1970. *The Structure of Scientific Revolutions,* 2nd ed. Chicago: University of Chicago Press.

Lancour, Harold. 1949/1971. Discussion. In *Education for Librarianship: Papers Presented at the Library Conference,University of Chicago, August 16–21, 1948,* ed. Bernard Berelson, 59–65. Rpt. Freeport, NY: Books for Libraries Press.

Leigh, Robert D. 1950. *The Public Library in the United States: The General Report of the Public Library Inquiry.* New York: Columbia University Press.

Library of Congress, Congressional Research Service. 1986. *Research Policies for the Social and Behavioral Sciences: Report.* Science policy study, no. 6. Washington, DC: U.S. GPO.

Lipset, Seymour Martin. 1996. *American Exceptionalism: A Double-Edged Sword.* New York: Norton.

MacArthur Research Network on Transitions to Adulthood and Chapin Hall Center for Children at the University of Chicago. 2005. *Adolescence and the Transition to Adulthood: Rethinking Public Policy for a New Century.* Philadelphia: MacArthur Research Network on Transitions to Adulthood and University of Pennsylvania.

Maines, David R., Jeffrey C. Bridger, and Jeffery T. Ulmer. 1996. Mythic facts and Park's pragmatism: On predecessor-selection and theorizing in human ecology. *Sociological Quarterly* 37, no. 3: 521–549.

Manley, Will. 1997. Patron revolt. *Booklist* 93 (1 May): 1464.

Matthew, Cynthia T., Anne T Cianciolo, and Robert J. Sternberg. 2005. *Developing Effective Military Leaders: Facilitating the Acquisition of Experience Based Tacit Knowledge.* Alexandria, VA: U.S. Army Research Institute for the Behavioral and Social Sciences.

McCabe, Ronald B. 2001. *Civic Librarianship: Renewing the Social Mission of the Public Library.* Lanham, MD: Scarecrow Press.

McGarry, Kevin. 2000. Professional education: Some reflections. *Education for Information* 18, no. 2/3: 105–113.

McKee, Bob. 2005. Futureproofing our professional association—convergence and CILIP. *Feliciter* 51 (2): 72–75.

McNally, Peter F. 2004. One hundred years of Canadian graduate education for library and information studies. *Feliciter* 50, no. 5: 208–211.

Mead, George Herbert. [1932] 1959. *The Philosophy of the Present.* LaSalle, IL: Open Court Publishing.

Merton, Robert King. 1968. *Social Theory and Social Structure.* New York: Free Press.

Mulvaney, John Philip, and Dan O'Connor. 2006. The crux of our crisis. *American Libraries* (June/July): 38–40.

Needham, George. 2006. Outline of presentation "The Library Education Conundrum" at the *Thinking Ahead Symposium.* Attachment to email to author January 9, 2007.

Neustadt, Richard E., and Ernest R. May. 1986. *Thinking in Time: The Uses of History for Decision Makers.* New York: Free Press.

Nicholas, Ralph W. 1991. Cultures in the curriculum. *Liberal Education* 77, no. 3 (May/June): 16–21.

O'Connor, Daniel, and J. Philip Mulvaney. 1996. LIS faculty research and expectations of the academic culture versus the needs of the practitioner. *Journal of Education for Library and Information Science* 37, no. 4 (fall): 306–316.

Ontario Library Association, Queen's University (Kingston, Ont.), People for Education. 2006. *School Libraries & Student Achievement in Ontario.* Toronto: Ontario Library Association. http://www.accessola.com/osla/graphics/eqao_pfe_study_2006.pdf.

Parker, Wendy L., Ward Bower, and Jane Weissman. 2002. Costs and benefits of practitioner certification or licensure for the solar industry. In IEEE Photovoltaic Specialists Conference. *Conference Record of the Twenty-Ninth IEEE Photovoltaic Specialists Conference, 2002: Hyatt Regency, New Orleans, Louisiana, May 19-24, 2002.* Piscataway, NJ: IEEE. Presentation available at http://www.irecusa.org/fileadmin/user_upload/WorkforceDevelopmentDocs/CertificationorLicensure.pdf (accessed July 13, 2007).

Perceptions of Libraries and Information Resources: A Report to the OCLC Membership. 2005. Principal contributors, Cathy De Rosa et al. Dublin, OH: OCLC Online Computer Library Center. http://www.oclc.org/reports/2005perceptions.htm (accessed September 22, 2006).

Peterson, Lorna. 2007. "Buffalo DLIS in UB Graduate School of Education." Archives of JESSE Open Lib/Info Sci Education Forum, March 2, 2007. http://listserv.utk.edu/cgi-bin/wa?A2=ind0702&L=jesse&T=0&P=8482 (accessed March 12, 2007).

Previte-Orton, Charles W. 1952. *The Shorter Cambridge Medieval History.* Vol. 1. *The Later Roman Empire to the Twelfth Century.* Cambridge: Cambridge University Press.

Public Agenda Foundation. 2006. *Long Overdue: A Fresh Look at Public Attitudes About Libraries in the 21st Century.* New York: Public Agenda. http://www.publicagenda.org/research/pdfs/long_overdue.pdf (accessed August 2, 2007).

Public Libraries in the United States of America: Their History, Condition, and Management. 1876. Ed. S. R. Warren and S. N. Clark. Special report, Department of the Interior, Bureau of Education. Parts I–II. Washington, DC: U.S. GPO.

Raber, Douglas. 1994. Inquiry as ideology: The politics of the public library inquiry. *Libraries and Culture* 29, no. 1 (winter): 49–60.

Raber, Douglas, and Mary Niles Maack. 1994. Scope background, and intellectual context of the Public Library Inquiry. *Libraries and Culture* 29, no. 1 (winter): 26–48.

Raymond, Boris. 1997. Chapter 1: Paradigms in conflict. In *Librarianship and the Information Paradigm*, ed. Richard Apostle and Boris Raymond, 1–36. Lanham, MD: Scarecrow Press.

Rayward, W. Boyd. 1996. The history and historiography of information science: Some reflections. *Information Processing & Management* 32, no. 1: 3–17.

Reece, Ernest J. 1936. *The Curriculum in Library Schools*. New York: Columbia University Press.

Robbins, Stephen P. 2003. *Organizational Behavior*, 10th ed. Upper Saddle River, NJ: Prentice Hall.

Ross, Catherine Sheldrick, Lynne (E.F.) McKechnie, and Paulette M. Rothbauer. 2006. *Reading Matters: What the Research Reveals about Reading, Libraries, and Community*. Westport, CT: Libraries Unlimited.

Rubin, Richard E. 2004. *Foundations of Library and Information Science*, 2nd ed. New York: Neal-Schuman.

Rudolph, Frederick. 1962/1990. *The American College and University: A History*. Rpt. Athens: University of George Press.

Samovar, Larry A., Richard E. Porter, and Edwin R. McDaniel. 2007. *Communication Between Cultures*, 6th ed. Belmont, CA: Thomson Wadsworth.

Saracevic, Tefko. 1994. Closing of library schools in North America: What role accreditation? *Libri* 44, no. 3 (September): 190–200.

———. 1999. Information science. *Journal of the American Society for Information Science* 50, no. 12 (October): 1051–1063.

Shiflett, Lee. 2006. Biographical statement. Biographical Statements for Conference Speakers. Fifteenth North Carolina Serials Conference—Crystal Clear? Today's Libraries, Tomorrow's Library Users, March 30–31, 2006. http://www.nccuslis .org/conted/serials2006/serials2006bios.htm (accessed March 8, 2007).

———. 2007. "Re: Buffalo DLIS in UB Graduate School of Education." Archives of JESSE Open Lib/Info Sci Education Forum, March 2, 2007. http://listserv.utk .edu/cgi-bin/wa?A2=ind0703&L=jesse&T=0&P=2505 (accessed March 7, 2007).

Singer, Benjamin D. 1996. Towards a sociology of standards: Problems of a criterial society. *Canadian Journal of Sociology* 21 (2): 203–221.

SLA (Special Libraries Association). *FAQ on Doing Business as SLA* http://www.sla .org/content/SLA/dbafaq.cfm (accessed February 5, 2007).

Squire, Kurt, and Constance Steinkuehler. 2005. Meet the gamers. *Library Journal* 130, no. 7 (15 April): 38–41.

Standards Review Committee, American Library Association Committee on Accreditation. 2006. Updating the 1992 *Standards for Accreditation of Master's*

Programs in Library and Information Studies: Overview and Comments. http://www.ala.org/ala/accreditation/prp/prismreports.htm (accessed December 19, 2006). Release approved by COA November 18, 2006.

Stigler, George J. 1971. The theory of economic regulation. *Bell Journal of Economics and Management Science* 2, no. 1 (spring): 3–21.

Summers, Ron, Charles Oppenheim, Jack Meadows, Cliff McKnight, and Margaret Kinnell. 1999. Information science in 2010. A Loughborough University view. *Journal of the American Society for Information Science* 50, no. 12 (October): 1153–1162.

Temporary Library Training Board, American Library Association. 1924. Report of the Temporary Library Training Board. *American Library Association Bulletin* 18: 257–288.

Thatcher, Margaret. 1992. Speech in the Hague ("Europe's Political Architecture"). The Hague, Netherlands, May 15, 1992. http://www.margaretthatcher.org/speeches/displaydocument.asp?docid=108296 (accessed March 27, 2007).

Upon the Objects to Be Attained by the Establishment of a Public Library: Report of the Trustees of the Public Library of the City of Boston, July 1852. Boston Public Library: 1852. City Document—No. 27 J.H. Eastburn, City Printer. http://www.scls.lib.wi.us/mcm/history/report_of_trustees.html (accessed December 11, 2006).

United States Department of Education, Secretary of Education's Commission on the Future of Higher Education. 2006. *A Test of Leadership: Charting the Future of U. S. Higher Education: A Report of the Commission Appointed by Secretary of Education Margaret Spellings.* Washington, DC: U.S. Department of Education. http://www.ed.gov/about/bdscomm/list/hiedfuture/reports.html (accessed December 22, 2006).

Warren, S. R., and S. N. Clark. 1876. Introduction. In *Public Libraries in the United States of America: Their History, Condition, and Management* (1876). Ed. S. R. Warren and S. N. Clark. Special report, Department of the Interior, Bureau of Education. Parts I–II. Washington, DC: U.S. GPO.

Webber, Sheila. 2003. Information science in 2003: A critique. *Journal of Information Science* 29, no. 4 (July 1): 311–330.

Weech, Terry L., and Marina Pluzhenskaia. 2005. LIS education and multidisciplinarity: An exploratory study. *Journal of Education for Library and Information Science* 46, no. 2 (spring): 154–164.

Whitson, Bill. 1995. Do we have a future? *CARL Newsletter* 18, no. 3 (September 1995). http://www.carl-acrl.org/Archives/ConferencesArchive/Conference95/future.html (accessed January 29, 2007).

Wiegand, Wayne A. 2001. Missing the real story: Where library and information science fails the library profession. In *The Readers' Advisor's Companion*, ed. Kenneth D. Shearer and Robert Burgin, 7–14. Englewood, CO: Libraries Unlimited.

———. 2003. To reposition a research agenda: What American Studies can teach the LIS community about the library I the life of the user. *Library Quarterly* 73, no. 4 (October): 369–382.

——. 2005. Critiquing the curriculum. *American Libraries* 36, no. 1 (January): 58, 60–61

Williams, Patrick. 1988. *The American Public Library and the Problem of Purpose.* Contributions in librarianship and information science, no. 62. New York: Greenwood Press.

Williamson, Charles Clarence. 1971. *The Williamson Reports of 1921 and 1923, Including "Training for Library Work" (1921) and "Training for Library Service" (1923).* Metuchen, NJ: Scarecrow Press.

Wilson, Louis R. 1936. The next fifty years. *Library Journal* 61, no. 7 (1 April): 255–260.

——. 1949/1971. Historical development of education for librarianship in the United States. In *Education for Librarianship: Papers Presented at the Library Conference, University of Chicago, August 16–21, 1948,* ed. Bernard Berelson, 44–59. Rpt. Freeport, NY: Books for Libraries Press.

Wilson, Patrick. 1983. *Second-Hand Knowledge: An Inquiry into Cognitive Authority.* Westport, CT: Greenwood Press.

Wingett, Yvonne. 2007. Gilbert library to be first to drop Dewey Decimal. *Arizona Republic,* May 30. http://www.azcentral.com/news/articles/0530nodewey0530 .html (accessed May 31, 2007).

Wolfle, Lee M. 1983. Prestige in American universities. *Research in Higher Education* 18, no. 4 (December): 455–472.

Index

About the Author

BILL CROWLEY worked for twenty-three years in New York, Alabama, Indiana, and Ohio libraries and library organizations in capacities ranging from part-time clerk to deputy state librarian. He earned a BA in history from Hunter College of the City University of New York, an MA in English from Ohio State University with a thesis in occupational folklore, an MS in library service from Columbia University, and a PhD in higher education at Ohio University in Athens, Ohio. Bill has published in the higher education, library science, and information science literatures, addressing diverse topics, including the competition between "library" and "information" in graduate education. Philosophically, he is a firm believer that academic theory should reflect the daily realities of the library, information, and knowledge worlds. He even published a 2005 monograph that addresses exactly this area entitled *Spanning the Theory-Practice Divide in Library and Information Science* (Lanham, MD: Scarecrow Press). More recently, Bill has begun to examine in print (both hard copy and electronically) the implications of unrealistically subsuming the primarily educational concerns and obligations of academic, public, and school libraries under an "information model" that is more applicable to the corporate and research sectors. He has explored the problematic consequences of such tactics for maintaining librarian professionalism in such recent works as "Suicide Prevention: Safeguarding the Future of the Professional Librarian," *Library Administration and Management* 20, no. 2 (Spring 2006), 75–80; "Save Professionalism," *Library Journal* (1 September, 2005), 46–48, and "Just Another Field?" *Library Journal* (1 November 2004), 44–46. Bill is now convinced that "information science" and "library science" have evolved into separate and equally praiseworthy fields that can be taught in the same program if library and information educators are sufficiently alert to the negative implications of attempting to subsume one under the other. He tries to keep this distinction in mind while teaching and researching as a professor with Dominican University's Graduate School of Library and Information Science.